The Philosophy of Ubuntu and the Origins of Democracy

Jeroen Zandberg

ISBN   978-1-4452-8234-3

NUR   754

Table of Content

Foreword

This book is the result of many years of participating in international politics and observing how political ideals offer hope to people in need but also noticing the despair when these ideals are unable to be implemented.

Many political leaders have genuine ideals of creating a better society and to help those who are unable to help themselves. Where it often goes wrong is the inability to achieve those ideals within the present system or be able to offer a viable alternative system. People consequently have the tendency to give up their struggle by either choosing to persevere in pursuing the wrong strategy or by turning their backs on politics all together.

With this book I hope to offer an insight into the workings and shortcomings of modern democracy in order to present a framework on how to build the best possible society thereby saving the community from oppression and giving them true freedom and opportunities.

The vision of society that I present in this book is based on my interpretation of human nature as developed from my studies of psychology and philosophy. In my opinion, any social system should reflect human nature if it wants to be considered a morally just system. Put differently, a system that does not reflect human nature is by definition an immoral system.

It is my conviction that the philosophy of Ubuntu is the best description of human nature and offers the best way on how society should be organised to maximize justice and human survival. I hope that the ideas in this publication will help people find new avenues for solving their problems and work towards a better future.

This book is a translation of several chapters of my 2009 publication called "The philosophy of new politics" (in Dutch: De filosofie van de nieuwe politiek).

Jeroen Zandberg

Introduction

This book deals with the African philosophy of Ubuntu and uses the latest insights into human nature to show how it can supplement modern thought on how to best organize society. An important aspect is that we will see that emotions are not the opposite of rationality but that emotions have rationality of themselves and that they are necessary for people to survive. Furthermore, we will investigate human morality and will see that it is based on our emotions and that it is for the most part innate. This consequently suggests that there are just a few limited possibilities for moral actions. Unfortunately, it does not mean that human action is always ethically just. An important section will be devoted to describing the exact location where morality is applicable, leading to the conclusion that everyone outside the 'Self' is also outside morality.

We will see that human rationality is based on the emotions and that it is not based in the atomised individual but in the *Self*, which consists of the social environment with which people identify.

The *Self* is not a blank slate and there are many innate abilities and potentials. We will look at the brain structures that enable us to be aware of ourselves and our existence. Every body part is for example represented in the somatosensory cortex by which we form an image of our own body. Furthermore, mirror neurons provide us an image of other people's thoughts. In this way we can build a framework of the workings of our *Self* that is further explained when we look at the studies into conformity and competition. People are by nature not directed at individual competition but instead directed at integration into a group with which people identify. The social environment with which people identify is part of the Self of that person. This human characteristic is an essential skill to survive in - and as - a human group, but can unfortunately also be abused.

The unconscious is of great importance for our daily thoughts and behaviours. Due to the fact that our consciousness is limited, many actions and thought processes will be dealt with automatically in the unconscious. Other people can manipulate these processes by strengthening and weakening certain thoughts. An example of this is *priming*, which means that specific information is offered to a person making him (unconsciously) think about it. The unconscious can be seen as a stairway to consciousness. When a thought rises above a certain threshold it will enter into consciousness, while it remains completely invisible to the consciousness when it is below this threshold. When we are confronted with a situation that can be interpreted multiple ways, the thought that is *primed* will enter consciousness while all other possibilities don't appear to exist. In this way manipulation is possible without a person being aware that he is manipulated.

This possibility for manipulation also has a major influence on the way in which we should see the human will. The will is only partially free when we look at it in a specific moment in time and space. There is however a possibility to have free will from a time perspective, because people can determine, to a degree, which processes are automatically running in the unconscious by actively learning these processes, after which they become automated. The great impact that the social environment has on our free will forces us to surround ourselves with people who have our best interests at heart and in mind.

We will see that a person is not an atomized individual who reasons from this solitary state. Instead a person is an integral part of the (social) environment with which he identifies. This *Self* is the basis from which people see the world and themselves. There is an innate tendency to recognize others as part of the *Self*. Disorders like Autism can block this recognition causing people to be closed off from others and thereby also closed off from themselves. The need for recognition is so great that it unconsciously takes precedence over other primary needs. This causes great danger when people lack proper recognition because other primary needs are pushed aside and people become more vulnerable to abuse. It can then even be the case that isolated people consciously seek conflicts in order not to wither away in isolation. There can after all be some recognition between people in a conflict.

Success of elites in society is mainly due to the labour of others. Forced labour only accounts for a small part of it. The most important mechanism in the persistence of this stratification is the manipulation of the will of others to desire something that goes against their own interests. By applying the insights we gained into human nature and the make-up of the *Self* in the first part of the book to society at large in the second part of the book we are able to uncover the possibility of manipulation of the will of people. Civilized behaviour plays an important role in this manipulation. The elite has for example civilized itself, meaning that they control their own emotions and oppress any aggressive and immoral tendencies. In light of the fact that human nature already is civilized suggests that this civilization does not build on a natural human condition but on a form of *uncivilization*. This uncivilization is imposed by the elite in order for them to rise above the rest of society. The elite then has the power and resources to rise above this uncivilization and to create a small layer of civilization. The rest of the population is manipulated to become uncivilized. This uncivilization is anti-intellectualistic and aggressive and keeps the less well off imprisoned by forcing them to display behaviour that goes against their interests. The imposition of civilization and uncivilization is only applicable in a society were there are no clear rules separating the elite from the rest of the population. Modern society offers people more potential freedoms and possibilities but it is only open to those who are on top. In the event that there is a separation between an elite and the rest of society the conclusion is justified that society is not open for all those who are not part of the elite. It is therefore essential in order to have an open society that everyone has a similar identity.

Western liberal democracy assumes people to be atomized individuals. The philosophy of Ubuntu on the other hand places the *Self* at its centre whereby the Self not only consists of the physical individual but also includes the social environment with which we identify. Without other people a person can never be fully human. Eastern philosophy also takes people and their social environment into its reasoning, but they place people as being part of their environment, while with Ubuntu the social environment is a part of people. This crucial difference makes for a completely different view of humanity and thereby also a different organisation of the best society.

According to the modern view of humanity, people can be complete persons as atomized individuals. Other people are then unnecessary and often seen as a limitation to the individual. With Ubuntu others are essential to become fully human. Others are then not a limitation but an expansion of possibilities. Ubuntu reasons from the Self, whereby the Self should be seen as the physical individual including everything with which he identifies.

The state of human nature includes the tendency of people to be directed at the recognition of others to become a full *Self*. Recognition by others is therefore a primary need, comparable to food and water, which are necessary to survive. In the following chapters we will see that people do not reason from pure individual interests, but that they always include a social environment that together forms the *Self*. Rationality therefore does not originate in the individual but in the *Self*. We will see that the philosophy of Ubuntu is therefore more rational then Western liberalism.

Besides superior rationality Ubuntu also offers solutions to social problems that Western liberal democracy can't solve without denying itself. Western liberal democracy for example states that a government should be elected by the majority of the population whereby it becomes their representative. The majority in a democracy is not formed by a physical majority of the people but by the majority in the public domain. Through debate in this public domain a certain Truth is formed that determines the direction of the government and society as a whole. The large influence of elite- and lobby groups in the West often enables small, well organised groups to promote policy that is not in the best interests of the physical majority.

The idea that the freedom of the people remains intact when there is the possibility to vote leaders out of office after they have implemented bad policy is often an illusion. The Truth in a democracy is after all determined by the debate in the public domain, which is primarily dominated by the political elite. In this way political leaders can create the truth themselves and is it possible that policy that is objectively bad for the population, but good for the political elite, is still supported by a majority. This democratic deficit is not present in Ubuntu. The core of the truth is in Ubuntu not formed by the winners of the debate in the public domain but by the interests of those with a similar identity. In a Western liberal democracy there is competition between elites who primarily identify with themselves and who each want to conquer the public domain at the expense of the other. This is not the case with Ubuntu because the public domain is determined by the identification with each other, making it impossible to have competing elites duelling for power. Due to the fact that the political elite share the same identity as the rest of the population makes for policy that is good for both. When the political elite stop identifying with the general population then Ubuntu disappears.

The philosophy of Ubuntu states that people are by nature directed at others and that they can only be fully human when they are recognized by others. Ubuntu therefore also provides for the best possible solution for the social contract theory. In Western- and Eastern philosophy all connections are enforced from the outside, causing a chicken-and-the-egg problem with social contract theories. These theories state that individuals close an agreement with each other in order to live together. Unfortunately a contract can only have value if there is already a morality present, but in both Western- and Eastern philosophy this morality is not innately present making it impossible to ever come to a contract. This problem is not present with Ubuntu because there is an innate tendency to recognize others as part of the *Self*. Furthermore, the social contract in Western philosophy assumes that individual freedom is sacrificed to enable co-existence. With Ubuntu there is no sacrifice of freedom. It actually increases with the size of the group. People are after all only fully human when recognized by others.

We will also see the great importance that self-confidence has in the success of people in modern society. Without self-confidence all off life's chances are only illusions. Self-confidence means to have confidence in your Self. In light of the fact that the Self is not limited to the atomized individual means that confidence can be boosted by being part of something successful. Great achievements by a government can then boost the self-confidence of people if they identify with this government. The same applies to cultural achievements as well and I hope that this book will contribute to the feeling of self-confidence in a philosophy that although innately human has African roots.

Happiness

The question what makes us happy is something the ancient Greek philosophers already debated over in the fourth century BCE. Especially Aristotle focussed on the causes of happiness and asked himself the question if happiness should be the objective of life. His philosophy has had tremendous influence on modern science and is studied and debated up till the present day. This is also the case for his view of what happiness is. Much psychological research has affirmed a lot of Aristotle's assumptions. To Aristotle human happiness is the objective of life. In order to be truly happy it is, according to Aristotle, necessary to achieve your full human potential. A truly happy life is not a life that revolves around fun and joy. Instead it is the life in which we maximize the use of our mental capabilities to excel in a job, task or activity making sure that we fully use our innate capabilities. Besides claiming that happiness is the objective of life Aristotle also claims that the individual life is an end in itself and that human life is not a means to reach a higher objective. This is something that Aristotle has in common with the later philosophy of Kant as well as the human rights lobbyists who also claim that people are an end in themselves and not a means to a higher objective.

Research into happiness

Science has seen great progress since the time of Aristotle. In our modern, scientifically based world any theory needs to be scientifically tested to gain acceptance as an explanation for a phenomenon. In case of happiness many studies have been done into the causes of happiness. One of the most extensive studies into happiness is the decade's long study of professor Veenhoven at the Erasmus University in Rotterdam. In this research people are regularly asked to rate their happiness on a scale from one to ten. A large amount of data has been collected from which it is possible to compare happiness in different countries and in different times. The country with the highest score in 2008 was Denmark with an average of 8.2. The top five is as follows: Switzerland is number two with a score of 8.1, followed by Austria with a score of 8.0. Iceland takes place four with 7.8 and Finland, Sweden and Australia share fifth place with a score of 7.7. According to this happiness research the Scandinavian and Alpine countries score the highest ratings, which could mean that people in those countries are happier than others. This opens up the question why some countries have more happiness than others. The unhappiest countries are to be found in Eastern Europe and Sub-Sahara Africa, while the happiest countries are in Northern- and Central Europe and South America. The thirty year study into happiness has led the researchers to several characteristics that predict if a country (or person) is happy. Firstly there is the need for a country to have a certain amount of wealth in order to have happy citizens. Furthermore, there needs to be a large degree of equality among the people of the country. It is also important that people are able to develop themselves, meaning that they have the ability to practice a useful profession and to be able to build a career. A (high) degree of individualism also determines to a large degree the high rating on happiness. These are the aspects that determine if a country scores high in the research on happiness.

Besides looking at international differences we can also look at what determines happiness on a micro-level. In that case we look at what determines the happiness of individual people compared to their neighbours, friends and colleagues. The results of this research show that people with too little money are unhappier than people with an average income, but that there is no significant difference in happiness after a certain level of wealth has been reached. This result has also been found in a comparison in time whereby the level of wealth increased but happiness continued to stay virtually the same. Happiness does however change when wealth rises for some and not for others. The increase in wealth of an elite is bad for the total happiness of society because the rich get a little happier while the rest becomes unhappier. This is because happiness is to a large extent relative and is compared to the situation of others. Inequality is therefore an important factor in a decline in happiness. The lower social position of many minorities might also be the reason why they are often unhappier than the rest of society. The good socio-economic position of Northern- and Central Europe in the international system might also have a large influence on the degree of happiness in those countries. Due to the fact that happiness is relative to that of others also means that the unhappiness of one can mean greater happiness for the other. Striving for happiness is therefore not always ethically correct. Another aspect that prominently comes to the fore in the research on happiness is the fact that happiness describes a personal situation, but that we can only be happy in a social community and in interaction with others. A final characteristic of happiness is to have expertise. There is a strong correlation between the measure of happiness and the measure of how good people are in their profession whereby it is also important that there is the possibility to act on the skills one has. These are the conclusions that were drawn from the studies on happiness.

Happiness in animals

Biology has made significant progress in showing the interconnectedness of biological systems and organisms since the general acceptance of the theory of evolution of Darwin in the 19th century. We now understand that humans and apes have a common ancestor who existed millions of years ago and that something similar also applies to all forms of life on earth. If we travel back in time far enough we will find a common ancestor for all species. The fact that people are part of the animal kingdom can also be used to study human behaviour by comparing it to animal behaviour. The fact that we use experiments on rats, apes and other animals to gain insight into human diseases also shows that people only differ from other animals in the amount of characteristics they have instead of differing in kind; they differ in degree and not in kind. We consider other animals as resembling people so we can validly test medications on them, but because we also consider them to be less in value we test it on them first before we attempt to do it on humans. When people only differ from other animals in the amount of the characteristics we all share than it is also possible to measure happiness in animals and compare that to the happiness in people.

There has also been extensive research into happiness in animals. Probably the biggest difference with the study of happiness in people is the fact that animals are unable to speak and thereby say if they are happy or unhappy. They are unable to fill in a form on Internet to rate their happiness. In order to circumvent this problem researchers use various observation methods of animal behaviour which they subsequently interpret to see how happy a particular animal is. In order to measure animal welfare and happiness, academics look at spontaneous signals that animals display. These signals are divided in *positive signals*, like looking for social contact, playing behaviour and curiosity to investigate new objects and *negative signals* like apathy, stereotypical behaviour, self-damaging behaviour, restlessness and disease. On the basis of the prevalence of these characteristics it is determined if an animal is happy or not. Afterwards researchers determined on the basis of simple tests what makes various animals happy. Like Aristotle already said about happiness in people is also the case for animals in that they are happier when they are able to perform their natural behaviour. For instance pigs are happier when they are able to grub in the dirt than if they are not able to do this. Animals are also happier when they are confronted with certain challenges in search for food than if they are simply handed the food. A certain degree of stress related to challenges increases happiness in animals. In order to gain maximum productivity in the agricultural sector it is crucial to find the right balance that makes animals happy. Finding the right balance is also applicable for happiness in people.

Depression

The people in Scandinavian countries are the happiest of all according to the research on happiness. Unfortunately this is not the only characteristic of Scandinavian countries because besides happiness they also score high on depression. It is even the case that if we leave out the poorest countries Scandinavia has the highest percentage of depressed people. Depression is in many respects the opposite of happiness. Where happiness consists of positive emotional signals which show that life is going well, depression consists of a collection of negative emotions that place a heavy burden on life.

Many explanations on the causes of depression have been tabled over the years. Today there is no general agreement on one all-encompassing theory that explains depression. Nonetheless there are some theories that are more accepted than others. The next group of explanations about depression is a selection of what in my opinion is best able to explain depression. Firstly there is the theory of *learned helplessness* as cause of depression. According to this theory people fall into a depression because they have learned that they have no control over their own life. The consequences of this helplessness are passivity and negative expectations about the future. In learned helplessness people were at one time exposed to a negative and threatening situation from which there was no escape. Following this event people subsequently think that it is impossible to escape in other situations as well even if objectively there is the possibility to escape. An important element in this psychological response is the belief that escape and avoidance of the negative situation is impossible thereby leading to a lack of motivation to escape from the situation. The subjective images about the situation are then a self-perpetuating prison. These incorrect images also decrease the possibility of learning that a new situation can also offer new possibilities and that the negative experiences are not universal but only applicable to a specific situation.

Another theory about what causes depression is closely related to learned helplessness in that it also looks into the subjective way in which people are aware of the world. This is the *cognitive social learning theory*. According to this theory, depression is caused by a sequence of negative expectations and convictions about oneself, the situation and the future. This dark outlook on life colours all experiences and possible decisions of a depressed person. It thereby becomes a prison in which people lock themselves up in a depression.

These two theories both assume that a negative outlook on life is the deciding factor that causes and maintains a depression.

The third theory about the cause of depression states that depression is the result of a decrease in stimuli from the environment. According to this behavioural theory the lack of positive social contacts causes people to decrease their activity and get a negative outlook on life. The decreasing social stimuli cause people to fall into a depression after which they retreat from social life and thereby causing depression to maintain itself.

What is striking about depression is that it is a self-perpetuating process. If a person has been made depressed at a certain time in his life, no external force is necessary to maintain this depression. The previous three theories on depression when combined are in my opinion a good explanation of depression.

Now that we have an overview of the probable causes of depression we can turn to the question why depression is so abundant in countries where people appear to be so happy. A first dent in this apparent contradiction is the fact that happiness is relative and that it is possible that the happiness of one can come at the expense of another. For example, the happiness of the majority can come at the expense of the minority or vice versa. Several clues to why depression is so abundant in Scandinavian countries can ironically also be taken from the research into happiness. According to the happiness research, individualism is correlated with happiness. As we noted in the overview of the causes of depression individualism can also lead to depression, because it can quickly lead to a decrease in positive social stimuli due to the fact that people live along side each other and not with each other. When people are unable to perform in an individualistic society they can quickly become marginalized and isolated. The emphasis on the individual and the dilution of family bonds can cause people to become isolated and easily fall into a depression.

Rationality of our emotions

When we talk about a life of happiness we do not refer to the possession of objective, worldly things but to a feeling we have. This is not to say that happiness can be entirely defined as a feeling, but that feelings, or emotions, form the basis of happiness. By discussing emotions we can make a distinction between an affect, mood, emotion and feeling-sensation. Affect is the most general of the four and is a subjective evaluation of something on a positive-negative scale and thereby encompasses the other three terms. A mood is an affective state which is not directed at a specific object, while an emotion on the other hand is directed at a specific object. Finally, feeling-sensations are stimuli that transmit information and are usually affective. Feeling-sensations can be divided in three categories. The first category of feeling-sensations is the physical sensations that provide us information about the body, like hunger and pain. The second category consists of cognitive sensations that provide us information about the knowledge we have of something, like surprise and confusion. The third category consists of affective sensations that provide us information about the status of our interests and objectives, like joy and sadness. Emotions always contain affective sensations and are thereby an indicator of the status of our interests.

What is the relation between reason and feeling? Are emotions rational, irrational or non-rational? Enlightenment philosophers, especially Kant, made a sharp distinction between the emotions and the ratio, in which the ratio was deemed superior. Just like the Stoics of ancient Greece there was even the ideal of banning emotions as much as possible because they were deemed harmful to the success of the individual and society. The reason why the Stoics were of the opinion that emotions should be banned or brought under strict control is the idea that emotions can overwhelm and deceive us whereby individual independence can be lost. According to this line of thought emotions are always harmful for us as a person and thus by definition irrational. This argument claims that emotions are not non-rational but that they reflect a wrong rationality. Besides feeling-sensations, our emotions also contain a reason that lies at the basis of these emotions that reflect our interests. This gives us indications on what we should prioritize. It is therefore wise to listen to our emotions because they warn us of danger and give us clues that we are on the right or wrong track.

We can discern more functions of emotions. Firstly there is the fact that an emotional response is faster than a cognitive response. For example, in case of danger, people will feel fear and have the urge to run away. This decision takes place in a fraction of a second. A cognitive response on the other hand will take much longer due to the fact that we then have to evaluate the situation and weigh the appropriate response. When a truck is racing towards us we will be squashed if we rely on a cognitive response and thoroughly analyze the situation before taking any action.

A second function of emotion lies in the social interaction with others. Through showing emotions other people get information about our situation and our vision of the world. This is essential for social organisation. The recognition of the other will be discussed in later chapters. Although most agree with the fact that people have emotions and that those emotions are related to events with which we are confronted, there is still no final agreement on how these emotions come about. The James-Lange theory for example states that an emotion is the result of an automatic feeling-sensation that comes about from a perceived stimulus. No higher brain activity is required to interpret the situation before we feel an emotion. With the Cannon-Bard theory the emotion only arises after a perceived stimulus is interpreted. Social research shows that both theories are (partially) correct and that there are two broad ways to feel an emotion, namely an automatic and a cognitive way, who supplement each other, but who can also occur separately.

There are clear indications that people become afraid automatically when confronted with certain stimuli and that this response is innate. Besides this, people can also become afraid as the result of an interpretation of a situation. The idea that there is nothing to fear but fear itself is therefore only partially true. Not all fear can be prevented and controlled by positively interpreting the situation. In the chapter about fear we will see that it is not possible to completely avoid the rise of fear and that an interpretation of the observed situation can not prevent it, because it circumvents consciousness. Thereby it is also the case that the best and sometimes only way to get rid of the feeling of fear is to create another emotion, namely aggression, and not through rational thinking. The fear response can on occasions completely circumvent consciousness. This means that we can then not decrease this fear by rationally thinking about the unconsciously perceived danger. Feelings of fear decrease the trust in others and in one's own ability to cope with the situation, thereby decreasing self-confidence. In light of the fact that self-confidence is a very important attribute to succeed in society and in life in general it is crucial that this problem is dealt with. Fortunately, human nature has through millennia of evolution evolved a mechanism to take away this fear as well as the cause of this fear. This mechanism is based on anger.

The most effective way to take away fear is by becoming angry. In this way there is an action-tendency to face the danger and oppression, whereby the feeling of fear, which can't be removed by rationally thinking about it, is replaced by anger and the fear actually evaporates. Anger is therefore a very important emotion if we do not wish to be paralyzed by fear which will cause us to descend into a depression and endanger our survival. Anger is therefore a good and essential emotion.

In a next chapter we will see that the Self is not limited to the physical person but that it also includes an environment and the persons within it. People can only become fully human if they are open to the other. This completion of the Self can not be solved by the ratio but works on the basis of the emotions as we will see with the discussion of autism, mirror neurons and the body image.

Emotions enable us to make faster decisions and in further chapters we will see that they play an important role in social interaction. Furthermore, our emotions provide us insights into the status of our interests and what should be prioritized to improve our living conditions. This characteristic of emotions grounds it deep in rationality. Without emotions, human rationality would not exist because we would not be able to see the importance of things and would be unable to make decisions. There would not even be any value because everything that is valuable to a person can be traced back to a feeling about something. Factual rationality can never provide such a value. Emotions are therefore not non-rational. They can be rational or irrational. They can interpret the world correctly or not, but they are rational. Emotions can be seen as opinions of value about the position of a person in the world.

Fear

Fear is probably the most essential emotion in our struggle for survival. It is an emotion that is very important but often seen as limiting and an emotion that we should ignore and/or suppress. This is an incorrect interpretation of the value of fear because the world really is dangerous and people are vulnerable. Our chances of survival would be minimal if we were to be completely devoid of fear. Fear of a lion is for example very rational because he is able to kill a person if the opportunity would arise. In such a situation it would be irrational to have no fear. The great importance of fear as a primary emotion can also be deduced from the fact that there are innate physiological reactions that automatically occur in response to certain stimuli that are a potential threat. We are for example *hard-wired* to have a fear response when a dark shadow comes over us. We are also hard wired to be scared of loud sounds. Fear can be the direct result of becoming aware of a dangerous situation. It can also be the result of an interpretation of possible danger. It is for example possible to be afraid of the tax collectors when you have a secret Swiss bank account. Despite the fact that fear can arise from an interpretation of the situation, not all fear responses are the result of conscious interpretation.

There are two ways in which fear is perceived, namely an automatic and a conscious manner. The automatic fear response completely circumvents consciousness. When a threatening stimulus (like a dark shadow) is perceived it goes directly to the parts of the brain called the *thalamus* and the *amygdala* without there being any conscious interpretation. Accuracy is hereby sacrificed for speed. Fast decisions are of course very important when confronted with a potentially life-threatening danger. It is better to be unnecessarily scared once than to once not notice a real danger, because you don't get a second chance. The second way in which fear is perceived does involve consciousness and thus interpretation. Although it increases accuracy it is also slower. Furthermore, this conscious observation is vulnerable to manipulation. Innocent events can be perceived as dangerous when people have been *primed* to interpret the situation in an incorrect way as we will see in a next chapter. Fear is thus a response to a threat. This can also be a perceived and non-existent threat. Because emotions are not simply physiological feelings but also include interpretations about the consequences of an event or situation for the person, there is the possibility that wrong interpretations are made. Fear can than be irrational. This is especially the case when the fear for something which is truly dangerous is generalised to situations which are not dangerous. Examples of this are fear of flying and fear of spiders. Although some spiders are dangerous to people most are harmless while people with arachnophobia fear all spiders. Fear of flying is also irrational because although a plane crash is usually fatal they are very rare and flying is still the safest form of transportation. The fact that fear can also be perceived unconsciously makes it hard to deal with phobias. Another form of irrational fear is panic. In the event that a person panics the result is that he looses control and doesn't know how to deal with the situation. In such an event there is a high probability that the wrong choices are made and that the person becomes a victim of the situation. The ability to feel fear increases our potential wellbeing and chances of survival. Without fear there can be no survival. It can however also overwhelm us or lead us to a misinterpretation of the situation. Furthermore, people who are less sensitive to fear can be a threat to society because they usually have a personality disorder; i.e. they are psychopathic. Psychopaths are pure egoists who can survive in modern society because the regulations and institutions needed to organize society provide them the ability to hide and profit.

Friendship, love, compassion and empathy

The ability to communicate emotions is also essential for friendship. With friendship it is necessary to have an emotional engagement with another person. This implies a need for trust between people. Trust provides people the secure environment needed to give something of themselves to others. Friendship also implies that there is a need for something from the other and that friendship is thereby a form of mutual dependency with positive effects for both parties. It will be impossible to establish a friendship when people are afraid to show their emotions. In case of a fearful environment their can be no access to the inner feelings of the other, excluding the ability for trust to evolve. This means that friendship is impossible in an environment of fear. Cooperation is a form of friendship that doesn't have to be equally deep for everyone.

Love, compassion and empathy are emotions which are directed at perceiving and constructing friendship and unity. These emotions are necessary to become a complete or whole person. Hereby it is not the atomized individual that should be seen as the elementary unit but the Self as we will see in later chapters. Love is related to friendship whereby it is a deepening of friendship. Love is an emotion that brings people closer together. *Being in love* is a form of physiological excitement directed at a specific person or object. Love encompasses more than just a physiological reaction and is also dependent upon interpretations.

Compassion and empathy are also directed at bringing people closer to each other. In a next chapter we will see that people have the innate tendency to conform to the opinion of others. Furthermore there is a strong need to be liked and thereby to be accepted by others who are part of our Self. This strong desire to be accepted by the group is probably the result of the vulnerability of people. Human babies are for example completely helpless for many years and dependent on their parents for survival. The need to bond is innate as it is with geese or apes. With people this need remains strong during our entire lifetime. It is even the case that people are unable to survive if they can't bond to someone or to something. These innate tendencies are therefore also a denial of the pyramid of Maslow which states that there is a hierarchy of needs whereby food and security are the primary needs before there is a need for self-actualisation and social bonding. Human nature proscribes the need for bonding as a primary need whereby ultimate survival is only possible if the 'top' of Maslow's pyramid is equally present to the bottom. The so-called top is therefore as important as the base for survival thereby denying the entire hierarchy of needs as detailed by Maslow. A real danger of abuse is present when people are not attached to something or someone. The innate need for recognition and the need for completion of the Self by including part of the social surroundings will be discussed in upcoming chapters. If we are completely isolated from relevant others and lack mutual recognition and don't have a complete Self then people will also look for recognition and empathy in a situation in which it is highly inappropriate and dangerous to try to incorporate those into the Self. In a situation in which others have the worst for us in mind than trying to recognize the other as equal is the worst possible strategy. Love and friendship in a small group is therefore essential for people not to fall victim to violence. Emotions like fear are not enough to safeguard against threats. Studies on groups in which people were forced to kill their best friend(s) show that it is not possible to properly function as a human being without a moral environment of mutual recognition. An enemy therefore has great interest in making sure that people are unable to create a full Self, because it will leave them far more vulnerable to attacks and abuse. In many instances the elite in a society are the most dangerous opponent of the general population because they try hard to break the bonds between people in order to simplify abuse. People don't just bond with other people but also to pets, lifeless objects and even to ideals. It is therefore possible to strengthen the Self against abuse by clinging to lofty ideals. The stronger a person's identity and personal Truth about life, the more he is able to defend against abuse and oppression.

Compassion and empathy have a strong neurological basis which is for the most part innate. It is however not the case that compassion and empathy are simply present in the brain at birth and that we don't have to put any effort into it. Compassion and empathy can to a certain extent be strengthened and cultivated and of course also suppressed. The neurological basis for the recognition of others is hardwired, but there are also higher processes that influence compassion and empathy for others. It is for example possible to consciously think about how it would be for a person to have a serious disease or if he is a victim of grave injustice. Hereby there is a possibility to identify with the other and thereby feel compassion. In this case it is very important to determine with whom there is identification and who is seen as the Other, because this determines who will be given empathy and who will be dehumanized.

Personality theories

Every person has a personality which consists of the characteristics that determine the way people interact with the world and how they perceive it and with which the person can be distinguished from others. The human mind is not a blank slate and there are many innate structures that determine what and how behaviour is learned and implemented. All people have innate abilities to learn language while the question which specific language is learned depends on the culture in which people grow up. Children who are completely isolated from other people and never come into contact with spoken language when being a child will never learn to speak even if at a later stage they come into contact with language, indicating that there is a specific window of opportunity to learn a language after which the ability disappears. The structure of a person's personality is innate but the environment is necessary to develop it.

At present several theories on the structure of the personality are accepted as presenting an insight into its workings. The various theories overlap and sometimes contradict each other without there being one definitive answer on how the personality works. What follows next is a summary of the most important theories about the personality and to what extent they are supported by empirical data.

One important theory about the workings of the human psyche was presented by Sigmund Freud and is called psychoanalyses. According to this theory the human psyche consists of three levels of consciousness: the conscious, preconscious and unconscious. Most of the mental activities take place in the area that we are not conscious about. Furthermore, Freud makes a distinction between the id, ego and superego which are according to Freud primarily located in the pre- and unconscious. The id is the basis of our psyche and is completely submerged in our unconscious. It is the source of motivation and operates according to the principle of desire which means that it strives for immediate gratification without taking the situation or other people into account. The id is primordial and not based on logical thought processes. The ego lies on top of the id and enables the primordial desires of the id to be attained in a social environment in which it is necessary to postpone gratification and attain objectives through logical reasoning. The ego can be considered the executive of the id. The weaker the ego, the more dominant the id, which leads to a person displaying primitive behaviour. Finally, the superego can be distinguished. The superego is located in all three levels of consciousness and acts as our moral guide and conscience. This conscience determines what we perceive as right and wrong and causes feelings of guilt and shame.

From this description of the human psyche Freud describes the various ways in which a person's personality develops. This development according to Freud goes through several psychosexual phases that have to be resolved in order to become a healthy adult personality. The individual personality is then created as a result of the resolution of the conflicts between the id, ego and superego. At the root of these conflicts stand the fears that arise out of the different desires of the personality. Freud distinguishes between the neurotic, moral and objective fear. The neurotic fear arises when a strong id dominates the weak ego whereby the primordial urges threaten to get the upper hand over the ratio. The moral fear arises from a strong superego dominating the ego whereby there is a feeling of sinfulness when one does not live up to the high standing ideals of the superego. The objective fear arises from the fact that the ego perceives a genuine threat.

Next, Freud named a number of defense mechanisms that the ego uses to protect itself from these fears. The most important defense mechanism is *repression* and can simply be described as to make effort to keep undesired thoughts out of our consciousness. The thoughts don't thereby disappear but continue to work in the unconscious. Oppression of child abuse is an example of this kind of oppression. The next defense mechanism is *denial* whereby unacceptable thoughts do enter consciousness but are denied as if they can not be true. The third defense mechanism is *rationalization* whereby unacceptable events are recognized but their emotional impact denied. Rationalization often takes the form of apologizing whereby a different and acceptable reason is given for a specific action while the event was in reality caused by another, unacceptable reason. The next defense mechanism is *projection* whereby we attribute unacceptable thoughts we have ourselves onto another person or group. The fifth defense mechanism is *reaction formation* whereby unacceptable thoughts are turned into their reversed. An example is to be extremely nice to a person you hate. The sixth defense mechanism is *displacement* whereby unacceptable thoughts are expressed in an innocent way, like hitting a punching bag if you feel aggression against a person. The final defense mechanism described by Freud is *sublimation* whereby the displacement of unacceptable thoughts is channeled to a certain activity that can deliver something good, like studying hard.

A second personality theory is the phenomenological approach which claims that the perception and the interpretation thereof forms the core of our personality. The subjective experience is than what forms the core of our personality. In order to find out what the personality is we need to know what the person feels and thinks. It appears as if the phenomenological approach sees the mind as a blank slate waiting to be filled with experiences. However, the fact that the theory talks of subjective experiences indicates that there is something that shapes and distorts the experiences. The phenomenological approach presupposes that the experiences are shaped in a way that people strive towards goodness and self-actualization whereby the objective is to reach our full potential. People would automatically grow to their maximum potential if there were no limitations. The theory does not state what this 'goodness' is and does not give an answer to what the personality actually consists of.

A third theory about the structure of the personality is a collection of theories collectively known as the personality-traits approach. A personality trait is in this approach a clearly definable and stable mental characteristic of a person. The personality can be organized in different traits which together form a unique personality. The most accepted personality trait theory is called the Big Five. The Big Five claims that there are five personality traits that together form a person's personality. These traits are: extraversion, conscientiousness, openness, neuroticism and openness. The theory has received a lot of empirical evidence and is found in many different cultures. People have the tendency to describe others and themselves in terms of the Big Five. It is however not clear whether these traits are innate or whether they come about as a result of the environment.

The fourth theory about the personality is the social learning theory which tries to describe the part of the personality which is learned. To this end the personality is described as a collection of learning processes. The first principle is called classical conditioning whereby a certain stimulus is associated with an emotional response through repetitive simultaneous occurrence of both. In this way a specific emotion can arise every time the associated stimulus is offered making it appear as if they are inextricably linked. A second learning principle is called instrumental learning and is based on reinforcement and punishment. Behaviours which are reinforced will be repeated while those which are punished will be displayed less frequently. Another learning principle is called observational learning whereby behaviour is influenced if we perceive the behaviour to be successful in others. The final learning principle is called cognitive social learning whereby the experiences are coloured by certain personality traits, comparable with the subjective experiences explained with the phenomenological approach.

There is a lot of overlap between the different personality theories and in other areas they complement each other. On the other hand no single theory provides a definitive answer to the question what the personality actually is. At present there is little empirical evidence to support Freud's theory of psychoanalyses although the idea that the unconscious plays an important role in our personality is generally accepted. The phenomenological approach bases its theory on the assumption that people strive for goodness and towards reaching our full potential. This has received little empirical evidence. The personality traits approach has on the other hand received substantial empirical evidence, especially the Big Five, but does not answer the question if the characteristics are innate or learned and is therefore more a descriptive theory than an explanatory theory. The social learning theory consists of different learning principles that each on its own have received a lot of empirical evidence but whereby it is not evident if these principles are at the base of creating our personality.

Recognizing others and our Self

Consciousness

Consciousness is the awareness of one's own existence. This awareness disappears when we are asleep or unconscious. The ability to have experiences and to meaningfully interact with the environment also disappears with unconsciousness. Consciousness is therefore a very important and precious commodity we can't do without. Although life without consciousness seems impossible, all of our machines lack consciousness, while at the same time they are able to perform many tasks far superior to humans. Examples of these are computers and robots. They are able to interact with the environment whereby they are aware of the environment through input from sensors after which they decide on the most appropriate action based on algorithms in their software. Even though they interact with the environment and can adapt their decision-pattern based on previous experiences we don't consider them to have consciousness. Computers are able to store and manipulate vast quantities of data far superior to the capabilities of humans. The main difference between humans and computers is the fact that computers store and manipulate data without knowledge about their meaning. Computers register facts while people register meaning. All thoughts and observations by people are *about* something, while the physical world never has meaning but is as it is.

There is a difference between consciousness and being conscious about something. The latter can be wrong, while the possibility of experiences that consciousness implies can never be wrong. An unanswered question remains if we can reduce consciousness to physical properties? Do we get consciousness if we replicate a human brain and if so do we know *how* it works? This question will probably not be answered within our lifetime. There are however many hypotheses about the workings and structure of consciousness, among which is the one put forward by Sigmund Freud. The organisation of human consciousness which is used in this book follows a division in four levels of consciousness. These are: the conscious, the pre-conscious, the unconscious and the non-conscious. The conscious is the 'location' where the external and internal events are located and to which we have access on a specific moment. The conscious can only hold a very limited amount of memories and thoughts at one specific moment. When we think of consciousness we usually refer to this conscious. The pre-conscious is the brain state in which thoughts can easily be brought into consciousness. The unconscious consists of those memories to which we don't have simple access but who can be brought into consciousness with some effort. The non-conscious however can never be brought into consciousness and consists of (the control of) physical processes. What consciousness exactly is remains a mystery up till today despite major leaps forward in neuroscience. The theory of Crick and Koch for example states that consciousness is created because the awareness of our senses comes together in time and thereby forms our consciousness. This 'coming together' happens when the neurons of our brain fire with a speed of 40 Hz. Even if this is true it would still not explain how such a physical process creates our subjective consciousness and why only brain cells create consciousness. At the moment we can only say that consciousness comes about under certain physical conditions but we are unable as yet to explain why this happens.

Body image

The previous page stated that consciousness is the awareness of one's own existence. An essential element in this is the way in which we are aware of our body. A person is not a brain in a vat but has a body with which it is in contact with the outside world. The question arises is how the brain is aware of the body in such a way that our mind perceives it as our own.

The brain's awareness of the body is localised in the somatosensory cortex. This cortex is located in the middle of the cerebral cortex and receives awareness of touch, pain and bodily position etcetera. Every body-part has a specific location in this cortex. The amount of brain mass that every part uses determines the sensitivity of this body part. For example the head and mouth cover almost fifty percent of this cortex from which can be deduced that these body parts are highly sensitive. The size of the cortex dedicated to a certain body-part is not related to the actual physical size of the specific body-part. It is also not the case that all representations of the body within the cortex are distributed as they are in the actual body. The thumb and the head are for example next to each other in the somatosensory cortex. Furthermore, the size and location of the different body-parts in the cortex are not 100 percent fixed. The brain has a certain degree of adaptability, called plasticity. For example, blind people who read Braille sometimes have an increased sensitivity of their fingers caused by the increase of their brain mass being associated with the awareness of the fingers. In most cases this increase in sensitivity means that other parts of the somatosensory cortex are taken over and the body parts previously associated with it become less sensitive.

A related phenomenon is the awareness of body-parts that are no longer present. This phenomenon deals with 'phantom limbs'. When a person looses an arm it sometimes happens that this person still feels the presence of that arm. This is partly caused by the fact that part of the brain which was aware of the arm is taken over by other body-parts in which stimuli from other parts of the body appear to come from the lost arm. The fact that the presence of phantom limbs sometimes also occurs in people who never had this body part indicates that there is an innate schema in the somatosensory cortex where each body part has a specific location. Although there is an innate blueprint for bodily awareness it nevertheless requires a lot of practice to get the proper body awareness. Babies take a long time to learn their bodies. Similar to other learning processes this will eventually become part of our unconscious. Adults therefore have an unconscious schema for the awareness of our body. Many things can go wrong in this process, which we will discuss in following chapters.

Mirror neurons

Babies need to learn their body to achieve a coherent self-image. Furthermore, in a similar way they also need to learn the social environment and incorporate it into the Self. In order to do this people need to learn to read other people's minds. Reading other people's minds is necessary and vital. If the mental life of one person were to be inaccessible to others there would be no possibility to communicate with other people because there could never be agreement on experiences and their meaning.

Evidence that there is an innate possibility to read other people's mind can amongst others be deduced from the innate possibility to learn language that every person has. Human language is an exclusively social phenomenon in that it has no meaning if we only take the individual into account. The correct question is therefore not *if* we can read other people's minds but *how* we do it. A major problem is the lack of a direct physical connection between us and other people. The thoughts of others are therefore not directly perceivable. Behaviour on the other hand is directly perceivable and herein lies the key to recognising the other as part of our-Self.

The behaviour we observe is interpreted and as a result we know what the other feels and thinks. This happens in a manner analogous to our own consciousness – we imagine what we would do in a similar situation. There are two theories that describe the workings of this process. The first theory states that we have a theory that connects the observed behaviour to certain mental states. This is therefore a *cognitive theory* in which we determine what the other thinks and feels based on logical deduction. The second theory is called the *simulation theory* in which we simulate the situation of the other person in our mind. Especially this second theory has received a lot of empirical evidence as correctly describing the workings of the brain. The key parts in this theory are the mirror neurons.

Over the last few decades neuroscience has discovered the existence of mirror neurons. These neurons become active when a person performs a task and are also activated when we see someone else perform a similar activity. Similar brain regions are activated when we observe an emotion with others just as when we feel the emotion ourselves. In this way we can feel what the other feels and think what they think. These are innate and automatic processes that enable our brain to be in direct contact with those of others without the need for a presence of a physical connection or paranormal senses. Specific brain regions are activated by certain thoughts.

When similar brain regions are activated when observing a task or emotion in others as when we ourselves perform the task raises the question how we can differentiate between our activities and those of others. Firstly, although similar brain regions are activated, the neurons usually fire more intense when we perform a task ourselves as opposed to seeing others perform it. This means that the difference is one of degree of activation. This is however an unreliable method to distinguish yourself from others and it might very well be possible to automatically react on activities you see with others but that don't relate to you. To counter this problem the brain has yet another mechanism that enables the separation between ourselves and others. Other neurons were discovered that interact with mirror neurons and in a way control them. These are called 'super mirror neurons'. These neurons are activated when people perform an act, but they don't fire when we see the act performed by someone else. Through the interaction between mirror neurons and super mirror neurons we know when we need to respond to an event if it pertains to us or if we should do nothing if it doesn't apply to us. If this interaction doesn't work properly we are in danger of having too little or too much identification with others. The next step in our investigation into the workings and structure of our Self is how we create meaning from the processes as described above. How do we connect causality to events and behaviour?

Conformity

The idea that an atomised individual does not represent a complete person can also be deduced from experiments that test the obedience of people. Probably the most famous experiment in obedience is the experiment of Milgram in the early 1960's. Test subjects were told by a research assistant to deliver shocks to a person sitting in another room who would have to answer questions. After every wrong answer the voltage of the shocks was increased, to a point that the person screamed in agony as a result of the electric shocks received. On authority of the research assistant the test subjects continued to deliver shocks after every wrong answer even when they would have been fatal. The test subjects were however not informed of the fact that they were the one tested and not the person in the other room who pretended to receive shocks but who in reality was an actor. This experiment intended to show that ordinary people will execute immoral and potentially life-threatening orders. The experiment confirmed that people are sensitive to authority. Many subsequent experiments reported similar results.

A related phenomenon is the strong tendency to conform to group pressure. While with obedience there is a sense of following orders, conformity does not rely on commands or hierarchy. People automatically conform to the behaviour of others without any explicit commands. In most cases this is done unconsciously in which we adopt the social behaviour of the group to which we want to belong. The classical experiment that showed the high level of pressure people feel to conform to the group was done by Asch in the 1950's. In this experiment, a test subject had to determine which line had the same length as a standard line. Three lines were presented of which two obviously were too long or too short. When the persons in the group in which the test subject was sitting all chose the line that was either too long or too short, the majority of the test subjects followed the judgment of the group and chose the wrong line. No-one made a wrong decision and everyone chose the correct line in the experimental control group in which a test subject had to decide without the presence of others. This was the most telling experiment on conformity, but many other experiments reported similar results. Further research indicated that people conform more in a larger group than in a small group whereby there was a rise in conformity until the group reached six to seven persons. Conformity also increased when the situation was unclear and when the group appeared to have expertise. The explanations for the strong conformity of people to the group are to be found in the desire to be correct and, more importantly, the desire to be part of the group. Conformity is an essential element of social interaction. A smooth conversation is impossible as is social life in general when people don't conform to the expectations of others. A conversation in which we can't anticipate the others' feelings and responses and which lacks mutual expectations will be full of uncomfortable silences. Similar to the innate ability to learn language, conformity is an innate ability and is essential for what it means to be human. Conformism is one of the crucial characteristics that have made humans master of the world.

Competition and motivation

People have many innate needs that ensure the survival of the person as an organism. There is for example the need for food. The motivation to still our hunger is one of the most primary needs of people and it helps us to survive. The need for sex is also a strong need but differs from the need for food in that the former is not necessary for the individual to survive. It is however essential for the survival of the genes of the person. Both hunger and the sex drive are primary needs. They are however not just influenced by the lower brain regions. For example, the body has innate mechanisms to maintain a natural weight balance. This means that in a normal environment the body will maintain a certain weight set-point whereby the desire to consume food is synchronized. Unfortunately there are many external factors, like social eating patterns and psychological factors like depression, that derail the body's natural ability to regulate its weight. This can lead to obesity and other eating disorders. Something similar can be seen with the regulation of the sex drive. Although hormones play an important role in sexual motivation there are also social influences and psychological factors that impact our sex drive. Furthermore, the recognition by and of others is also a primary need. A lack of recognition causes serious psychological and physical problems which can't be resolved by taking care of other needs. People always have a need for recognition just as there is always a need for food.

The need or motivation that this chapter looks into is whether the motivation to achieve and consequently to gain power is innate or learned. This question is related to the previous investigation into conformity. Is competition innate and is there a will to power? We have already concluded that the desire to conform to the group is very strong. This alone already indicates that individualistic competition and a will to power is probably not part of the state of human nature. This leaves us with the motivation to achieve as main argument to see if competition is part of the state of human nature or that it is a result of external influences. Like many social psychological studies the most extensive investigation into competition has been done in America. Americans see themselves as highly competitive and born to achieve, which has led to much research into competition and the motivation to achieve. The focus of these studies is the question whether the motivation to achieve is innate or learned and to what degree other cultures are competitive. When we jump to the conclusions of these studies we see that they indicate that the motivation to achieve is primarily learned and not innate. This conclusion is reached amongst others by the fact that the motivation to achieve varies considerably between cultures and through time. It became clear that the motivation to achieve is correlated with the emphasis that education places on the value of performance. The fact that people from non-performance oriented cultures from Africa and South America were able to get a significant rise in their motivation to achieve after they received training courses indicates that the motivation to achieve can be learned. The motivation to achieve can be learned through training that encourages people to achieve. It is however not necessary to teach people to be non-achievement oriented. People will be non-achievement oriented when the educational system and society as a whole don't encourage people to be competitive. When we combine these results with the strong inclination to conform to the group we can come to the conclusion that the idea of competition, in the sense of an individual will to power, does not exist in the state of human nature and that it is learned instead of innate.

The motivation to achieve can be divided in intrinsic- and external motivation. According to the most common theory intrinsic motivation means that a person wants to perform a task because of the task itself, while external motivation means that a person performs a task in order to get something else. A high motivation to achieve is often connected to intrinsic motivation, which is the reason why the latter has a high value in western society. Is some-one ever really motivated to perform a task only for the task itself or are there other motives? Performing a task just for the task itself is the epitome of senselessness. A task therefore always has a purpose. If the task does not help to achieve the ultimate goal of life, which is survival, than it is a harmful activity and should be stopped. If there is a motivation to achieve it will always be directed at (perceived) improvement of the position of the person; i.e. the increase of survival of the genes. With intrinsic motivation people have the sense that the task, and the always present objective of that task, directly contributes to this survival, while with external motivation the task is seen as a way to gain access to another task that will guarantee survival. In that sense external motivation is a characteristic of a person in an oppressed social position. When people are in an oppressed position it is very difficult to make the correct choice which task you should focus on to get out of that situation. Intrinsic motivation is usually associated with endurance and faith in one's own abilities while external motivation is associated with fear of failure. With external motivation people attribute success to external factors that are beyond the control of the person and at the same time attribute failure to internal stable factors. All these characteristics make it difficult for a person with external motivation to succeed. It furthermore creates a high probability of falling into a depression.

Automatism and the unconscious

What makes us a unique person? Is it our thoughts, memories and attitudes? In the previous discussion on consciousness we divided mental processes in four different states. The conscious, what we are aware of at any moment in time, is very limited and can not hold more than one thought or activity at a time. Despite these limitations we are able to perform many complex activities at the same time. The key to this ability lies in the pre-conscious and unconscious. Complex mental processes can almost completely be performed by the unconscious. This gives the conscious the freedom to perform those activities that as yet can not be performed by the unconscious. This ability is called automatism. The more we are able to do automatically, the more cognitive resources we have available for other tasks. There are more advantages of automatic mental processes. If we wish to excel at something, than this process should, at least partially, be automatic. When does a mental process become automatic? A process becomes automatic through practice and the way in which this happens indicates that the automation of mental processes is most likely an innate ability. Automation goes rapidly and automatic and the only thing that is necessary is repetition of the process.

A psychological process is automatic if it runs unconsciously, or does not require attention, or does not intentionally start, or is difficult to steer. This is contrary to a controllable mental process that is located in our conscious. The division between an automatic- and controllable process is in reality not so distinct, because the conscious, pre-conscious and unconscious flow into each other without clear boundaries separating them. Automatism of mental processes can also be subdivided analogous to the division of consciousness,. Firstly, there is the pre-conscious automatism, which can be seen as the purest form of automatism. This includes automatic processes that start as a result of stimuli that are unconsciously perceived. This is especially true for stereotypes and chronically accessible constructs. The second form of automatism is post-conscious automatism in which the unconscious process is started after a stimulus has entered our consciousness. The process is started within the conscious but then disappears to the background and remains active in the unconscious. The third form of automatism is *goal-dependent automatism*, which means that a process is only activated under specific circumstances and when it is directed at a specific objective.

The limited capacity of our consciousness means that we are unable to process all information that reaches us. This safeguards us from being overwhelmed by useless sensations. Fortunately we have the innate ability to focus our attention on specific stimuli. By focussing our attention we are able to filter out one stimulus in a large group of related stimuli and in that way we select what enters our consciousness. There are various theories on how this selection process works. One theory is the *filter theory* which states that stimuli are filtered at the level of the senses. Other theories state that the selection process is less rigorous or definitive and that we also perceive sensations that do not enter consciousness. This theory is known as the *late selection theory*, which states that stimuli are not filtered on the level of the senses but that they are first interpreted. The selection process to determine which sensations will enter consciousness takes place in the unconscious, according to the late selection theory. The unconscious determines to a large degree what enters our consciousness. An example that supports the late selection theory is the cocktail party phenomenon. During a (cocktail)party we are able to have a conversation with a small group of people because we ignore the background sounds. However, when someone in the room suddenly calls out our name we immediately focus on this sound. This phenomenon shows that the stimuli we ignore are still to a degree perceived and that our name was instrumental in switching our focus. Our name is one of the most effective ways to get our attention because it is almost always automatically processed by our unconscious and subsequently brought into consciousness.

Schemas are one of the underlying mechanisms on how we perceive the world, what information we select and how we connect them to each other. Schemas consist of a collection of knowledge and judgments about a stimulus. With the aid of schemas we select, order and store information as well as associate it with previous information. Schemas are crucial in how we see the world. They are responsible for the fact that we organise the perception of the world according to our expectations.

One of the most important phenomena in which schemas, the unconscious and automatisms come together is in the special schema called *chronically accessible constructs*. These are characteristics that are central to the way a person thinks about himself and others. They are easily accessible in our memory. Previously we noted that consciousness is limited and that therefore few stimuli are able to reach consciousness at a specific time. Problems can arise from this limitation, especially in situations which are open to multiple interpretations. For example a person displays a certain behaviour that can be interpreted in multiple ways. What interpretation will we choose? The unconscious plays a crucial role in this process. We assume that many properties can be associated with the behaviour we observe. These properties are all in our unconscious and are thus not visible in our consciousness. Although the properties are all located in the unconscious they all have a different level of activation. A good comparison is a staircase leading to the conscious in which every property is located on a different step. A property enters consciousness when it crosses an activation threshold after which it is activated. When we observe a behaviour that is equally associated with a group of properties in our unconscious than they will all be activated in the unconscious. The property that is located at the highest step of the staircase to our consciousness will cross the activation threshold and thereby enter consciousness. The level of activation of a property in our unconscious is determined by two factors. Firstly, whether it has been activated recently and secondly whether it was activated frequently. The more recent and frequent the activation, the higher the property is on the staircase to consciousness. These processes are fully automated and we are unaware of what other possible properties we could have chosen. It appears as if the chosen property is the only correct choice and that it is inextricably bound to the observed behaviour. We are unaware that the other properties are similarly associated with the behaviour because they had a lower level of activation in our unconscious and therefore didn't enter consciousness. What factors determine whether a property is chronically accessible? One factor is the degree in which the Self-schema sees the properties as integral to our self-image. The properties strongly connected to the way we see ourselves are also used to judge others. Furthermore, it is also the case that the accessibility of a property is a self-perpetuating process because every time a property is activated it will get a higher level of activation and therefore will have a greater chance of coming into consciousness. Finally, properties that according to our *implicit personality theory* are associated with the chronically accessible property will be activated themselves and therefore also become chronically accessible.

An effect related to chronically accessible constructs is the *rebound effect*. This effect states that thoughts we consciously oppress will return stronger and more often after they are no longer oppressed. The rebound effect is caused by the fact that two different processes are at play when you try to oppress a thought. The first is the *operating process* which looks for stimuli that are not related to the oppressed thought, causing us to think of other things. The second process is the *monitoring process* which looks for the oppressed thought and makes sure it is not activated and stays oppressed. As we noticed with the discussion on chronically accessible constructs, a thought that is activated more often will have a higher level of activation in the unconscious and therefore have a greater chance of being activated next time round. At a certain level the monitoring process activates the to-be-oppressed thought causing it to attain a higher level of activation in our unconscious. Furthermore, the monitoring process is automatic and therefore can be performed by the unconscious while the operating process is not automatic and has to be controlled by our will. The monitoring process will automatically continue because it is automatic and doesn't need conscious control when we have to perform another task or if we have to perform multiple tasks at the same time. The operating process on the other hand will be stopped because there is no available space in our consciousness to control the process. The result will be that the forbidden thoughts will become stronger and activated more often. In this way thoughts that are oppressed will become stronger and more frequent causing them to play a greater role in how we interpret the world around us. Due to the fact that the oppressed thoughts have a higher level of activation they will be used more often in interpreting observed behaviour with others and ourselves as well as with the situation. The irony of control is therefore that we achieve exactly the opposite of what we intend to achieve. Individual control over our consciousness is therefore not as absolute as we might have hoped.

Another aspect that undermines the perceived control over our own thoughts and mind is the principle of *priming*. With priming, a schema or property is activated by a *prime* (= a stimulus), causing the person to use a particular schema in his interpretation of the observed behaviour or situation. In this way it is possible that someone might have a negative stereotype about a certain population group. This stereotype can be activated by a certain event after which the stereotype can then be used to judge another situation that is not directly related. The stereotype would probably not have been used in the latter situation had it not been primed. Our dependence on the surrounding (social) environment on what enters our consciousness is potentially dangerous and can lead to abuse and oppression.

In the previous pages we noted that our thoughts are often not really our own and that what enters our consciousness often escapes our conscious control. Something similar applies to our behaviour. The behaviour we display is only partially caused by a deliberate choice to behave in that particular way. Our attitude determines only a small part of our behaviour. The best prediction of our behaviour is to look at what behaviour we displayed in the past. The same principles that were at play with the automating of thought processes also apply to behaviour. Through frequent repetition behaviour becomes automated, i.e. a habit. This is called habitual behaviour. Behaviour that is often repeated becomes stronger. Habitual behaviour is unconscious and a form of goal-dependent automatism, which means that when we are confronted with a certain objective we automatically display the behaviour that is associated with this objective, without any conscious effort. For example we might have developed the habit to take the car when we go shopping. When one day we notice that we have no more bread at home we might decide to go the shop. Although the bakery might be 500 meter from our house we will automatically grab the car even if walking or cycling would be faster and more efficient..

Autistic disorders

When people have an autism disorder something goes wrong in the perception of others and the perception of experience. This disorder causes an inability to form genuine social contacts with others and therefore autistic persons are isolated from others. Due to the fact that people are by nature social beings and success and happiness are only to be found within a community this disorder has major consequences. The position in this book is that autism (and related disorders like ADHD and Asperger) are not caused by a genetic disposition but caused by a dangerous, undermining and hostile environment. The arguments to support this argument can for example be found in the obsessive control which is an important characteristic of autistic behaviour. Autistics panic when they are in an unstructured situation. They try to overcome this fear by excessive control of themselves and the situation. The environment is perceived to be so dangerous that the only way to confront it and survive is to implement a range of rules upon the person itself. It is therefore comparable to a bureaucratic organisation that has a large number of rules to protect itself from abuse. Another characteristic of autism is the fact that social contacts are difficult to create and that friendship is therefore almost impossible. In order to have friendship people need to be open towards others which makes people more vulnerable to abuse. An explanation that is often provided to account for the bad communicative skills of autistics is that they are unable to imagine themselves in other person's shoes and that they therefore have no empathy. An encounter with an autistics is than always formal and detached. Another sign that autism is a reaction to a hostile environment comes to the fore in circumstances where autism suddenly appears to vanish. Autistics usually open up in contact with animals and are able to interact with them. The fact that autistics are able to have social behaviour towards horses and not towards people gives a clear indication that it is not the ability to imagine other people's feelings and individual social skills by themselves that are broken, but that it is the situation that causes the autism. A horse is not threatening while a person can be. The fact that the narrowing of consciousness is a characteristic of autism also gives an indication that it is a reaction to a perceived threat. When a 'normal' person is confronted with a stressing situation in which he is psychologically attacked he will also experience a narrowing of consciousness similar to that seen with autistics. Autism can therefore best be seen as a (normal?) reaction to a dangerous and threatening situation. This hostile situation is dealt with by implementing a strict set of rules upon oneself. This means that there is a struggle for power in which the autistics will try to control his world in which the other is only a pawn. When autistic persons specialize in a narrow scientific field they are often able to gather a lot of expertise and power. An example is a professor who becomes the world authority in his field of study but who is also socially inadequate.

Attention Deficit/Hyperactivity Disorder (ADHD) is related to autism, but has several additional characteristics. A person suffering from ADHD is unable to concentrate on the important things in life like getting a good education. A lack of education combined with bad social skills and a limited personal world cause people to become unhappy and unsuccessful in life. The person who suffers from ADHD has even lost his motivation to try and become happy. This means that the person with ADHD is often in an even worse situation than those with 'normal' autism. Not all egocentric behaviour should however be characterised as autistic or as

ADHD. In many instances the autistic and ADHD behaviour can better be seen as a strategy in the competition for an important social position and as a will to power at the expense of the other. When a person claims to suffer from an autistic disorder and ADHD while he at the same time competes for an important social position in the community than it is usually a will to power. A true autistic would not notice the social demands or would not even have the desire to attain the social position. In light of the fact that this competition is almost always present leads to the conclusion that autism is usually a will to power by a person who is oppressed.

In preceding pages we encountered elements that diminish the chances of a good and happy life. We also noted why these strategies are used even if they are self-defeating. An important element in depression is the lack of motivation for action and a strong form of helplessness that keeps people imprisoned. Self-handicapping, autism and even physical self-mutilation are all methods to gain some control over one's own life. To have control over one's own life is an important factor in the amount of happiness. People who have control over their life are happier and less often depressed. This is even the case when the control is only imaginary. When control is only imaginary we talk of superstition. An example of such superstition is the idea that wearing red socks on an airplane will guarantee that the plane will not crash. The amount of control also influences the physical health of people. People who think that they have control over their life and situation have a better immune system compared to those without control. Although self-mutilation is a negative thing we can also conclude that it is not without objective. The objective hereby is to be found in preventing an even greater loss/damage by pretending to control one's own life. Self-mutilation than becomes a form of self-control. Of course this is a self-destructive and unwise method to gain control over one's own life and hopefully this book will offer better ways to get self-control.

There are many indications that presently a happy and successful life are harder to reach for an ever expanding part of the population. For example, when comparing the situation with twenty years ago there is a large increase in psychological disorders that hamper the ability to function successfully in society. One of these is autism that is currently diagnosed far more frequently than before. A characteristic of autism is that people try obsessively to control one's own thoughts. Another characteristic of autism is the frequent repetition of behaviour which appears to be pointless. Flattening of emotions and decreased ability to imagine other people's minds are additional characteristics of autism. Finally, autism makes it more difficult to consciously focus attention and it narrows the consciousness. Autism is often diagnosed in childhood which led some to conclude that (the vulnerability for) autism is innate. The fact that autism is diagnosed far more frequently then before makes this unlikely. The increase in autism could of course also be related to a more competitive society that influences both the parents as well as their children.

In the investigation into the workings of the body image and mirror neurons we noted that children need to learn the awareness of their own body and the minds of other people. The awareness of others is made more difficult when suffering from an autistic disorder. The fact that people are social creatures means that the inability to imagine other people's minds is comparable to the lack of feeling in one's own body. As described in the chapter on mirror neurons people who do not suffer from an autistic disorder will have a simulation taking place in their brain when they see another person in a specific situation. We simulate the situation of the other in our own mind as if we were the one in that particular situation. Supporting evidence for the working of mirror neurons is in part derived from studies with autistics. The classical test to see if people are able to imagine other people's minds consists of the following scenario. A test subject sees a short film in which person A puts a cookie in the cookie jar and subsequently leaves the room. Next another person comes in and takes the cookie out of the jar and places it in the cupboard. Finally, person A enters the room again. The question now is where person A will look for the cookie? In the cookie jar or in the cupboard? Children younger than four years of age think that he will look in the cupboard because they assume he has the same information they have. The child saw that the cookie was taken from the cookie jar and placed in the cupboard so the child assumes that person A also has this information. At about four years of age normal children understand that the person doesn't know that the cookie has been moved. Children with Down syndrome also pass this test but children with autistic disorder don't. In other tests where intelligence and cognitive abilities are measured autistic children score comparable marks to normal children while children with Down syndrome score poorly. This is a strong indication that imagining other people's minds works via the simulation theory and that the cognitive theory is therefore incorrect. If the cognitive theory were correct autistic children would pass the test while children with Down syndrome would fail. The main problem with autistics is not a lack of intelligence but that they are unable to read other people's minds and are therefore unable to make connections with the social environment. The obsession with control and the narrowing of consciousness are also characteristics you would expect from a person who is threatened and under great stress. Autism can therefore be a reaction to a hostile environment in which the child is unable to open up to others out of fear and consequently is imprisoned in his own small world. The characteristics of autism can furthermore also be seen as a sign of egocentric behaviour and a will to power in which the lack of empathy, the flattening of emotions and obsessive control can rationalise oppression and make it easier to abuse others.

The will

An essential building block of our modern democratic society is the idea that we have a free will. People are than free to make their own decisions about life's choices. In previous pages we noted that many psychological characteristics draw the free will into question. In many cases the free will is less free than we might wish. This however doesn't mean that the free will doesn't exist. It only implies that free will is not absolute and that when we wish to have a truly free will we have to work hard for it. We have seen that our consciousness can roughly be divided in a conscious and an unconscious and that the conscious is only able to process a limited amount of information at the same time. A large part of our observations circumvent our conscious and are automatically processed by our unconscious. The essence of free will is that thoughts and decisions are intentional and under control. According to this formulation everything that is processed by the unconscious doesn't qualify for a free will. Although this might appear a logical conclusion it is in the end incorrect. This is due to the fact that consciousness is not so much localized in place as that it is localized in time, meaning that many conscious processes are the result of unconscious processes. The question than arises how automatic processes taking place in the unconscious are compatible with free will. Firstly, we are able to measure the brain activity which predicts what the eventual decision is going to be before a conscious decision is made. The unconscious processes therefore prepare the decision. Schemas play a major role in this process. As noted previously, schemas determine to a large extent how information is processed and saved. These schemas are learned from experiences about the world and the interpretation thereof which are stored in schemas. By consciously thinking about a particular situation we are able to adapt the schemas we already have about this situation to better suit our needs. This means that unconscious automatic processes are in a way also under the control of our free will. The difference is the localization in time. Free will can be present before the occurrences of automatic processes (meaning that we are able to adapt our general thoughts consciously) and also after the automatic processes have taken place as a product of which we can steer the results. From this perspective, free will is not something that takes place once and in isolation but encompasses a (life-)long process.

It is not difficult to see that the free will has to overcome many obstacles to be truly free and remain free. Abuse and oppression by others are real dangers. Firstly, we are confronted with the fact that the free will is limited because it requires cognitive effort from the conscious whereby we know that the conscious can only hold a limited amount of information at a time. It is therefore relatively easy to overwhelm the will. The will is limited and therefore able to hold only a limited amount of information. When we control some thoughts we are unable to control other thoughts because our conscious is 'full'. In such an event we are more vulnerable to abuse. Controlling and oppressing certain thoughts makes it more difficult to oppress other thoughts. In the previous discussion on the control of our thoughts and behaviour we also noted that control often works against us. Oppressed thoughts get a higher activation in our unconscious which makes them increasingly difficult to oppress. In the event that we are forced to control certain thoughts we are faced with the situation that we are more vulnerable to attacks by way of other thoughts that can (automatically) determine our behaviour through the unconscious. In such cases we have no free will and are (partially) at the mercy of others or the situation. This is however not the same as breaking the will. It is questionable if it is even possible to actively break the will without shutting down the conscious.

The principle of *priming* makes a potentially dangerous situation even worse. As we previously noted priming works by offering a stimulus (or *prime*) that activates certain schemas and thoughts whereby they reach a higher level of activation in the unconscious and are therefore more often used in the interpretation of the situation. When our consciousness is actively oppressing certain thoughts then the unconscious will process other stimuli. If the unconscious is primed with harmful schemas than these will automatically be used to interpret the situation and subsequently automatically influence our behaviour. In this way we can loose much of our free will to the situation and to other people. We then loose control over our own will. The idea of the 'will to power' has to been seen in this light. The will to power of the person who is oppressed is aimed at regaining control over his own thoughts. The will to power of the other is directed at making oppression as strong and extensive as possible. The will to power over others is most likely not a natural, innate characteristic as we can deduce from our knowledge about conformity and competition. The will to power over others is therefore more a reaction to an individualistic, competitive society that stimulates this behaviour because it can offer greater success to some, at the expense of others.

How can we make our free will as free as possible? When answering this question we have to include in the definition of the free will controlled intentions that eventually offer a positive outcome for us. Previously we noted that thoughts consist of subjective experiences about something and behaviour is caused by reasons emanating from these thoughts in order to display this behaviour. The fact that we are human and subject to the physical laws of nature means that we have to take these into account. When we leave quantum mechanics out of the equation which state that the universe is statistical rather than deterministic, we can state that we live in a world where all causes have effects and that we therefore live in a deterministic world. If all events happen as a result of previous events then the question arises whether we actually have free will and when we have it. Mental reasons are a form of causes, which means that they in turn are caused by previous mental events in our unconscious and the environment. This doesn't mean that we therefore are unable to influence this chain of events. Although effects are the result of previous events it doesn't mean that it was pre-determined. A result is not automatically pre-destined. We have the ability to influence this chain of events, but as we noted previously regarding the abuse of our will, this is a difficult process when we find ourselves in a hostile environment. What is the most important element that determines if we have a free will or not? It is for example possible to be 'free' to display behaviour as well as be 'free' in our thoughts without us having a free will, because as we saw in the discussion on priming and activation of thoughts in our mind we can be influenced, abused and manipulated by others and the situation. It is therefore also possible that we desire something that we don't desire ourselves but which is forced upon us. We than desire something that others want us to desire. It is subsequently possible that we desire something that goes against our interests. In light of the fact that the free will should be at the service of the objective of life, i.e. survival, we can conclude that we can only be free if the thing we desire is what we desire ourselves. As long as we have the freedom to test our desires and the ability to adapt them where possible we can be considered free and have a free will even if we live in a deterministic universe. Only when we come to the level of the principles of evolution is the idea of the free will limited.

The free will is thus not only dependent on one time decisions in our conscious, but is the result of continual adaptation of our thoughts and feelings that are for the most part resident in our unconscious. Through reflection on what is good for us we have to determine whether these thoughts and feelings are in our best interest. If they are not in our best interest than we should try to adapt them. This process of planning, control and adaptation enables us to have a high amount of free will and to be able to make correct assessments of the world around us. The major impact the world and the people around us have on the well functioning of our Self, also indicates that we should find an environment that is friendly and is directed towards our best interest. In a hostile environment it will be very difficult to cultivate a free will.

A preliminary image of the Self

Probably the most important thing we can say about the Self is that we don't know everything yet and that there remains uncertainty on crucial elements. It is for example still unanswered what consciousness actually is. What is it to have consciousness? What does it mean to be human a dog or an elephant? We know a lot about the elementary building blocks of the brain and how they work. The make-up of neurons and the way in which they communicate via electro-chemical signals is relatively well known. The workings of the higher cognitive functions are also increasingly understood. Modern brain scanning techniques make the thought processes visible. An important open question remains how we go from the building blocks to the building itself or differently put, how do we go from the syntax to the semantics? We know that consciousness is not localized in location but in time and that integration of different processes in the brain leads to consciousness. The major role of unconscious processes has been described in previous pages. These processes have a major impact on the way in which we see the world and how we react to it. They determine to a large extent our identity. It is also worth mentioning that our psychological make-up is not a clean slate that has to be filled by events from the environment. The brain contains many functions that determine what it means to be human. For example, the brain has innate structures that determine how we perceive our own body. It however costs time and effort to correctly develop these structures and there is always the chance that something goes wrong. Most information on how the brain works has therefore been obtained by studying those cases in which something went wrong. The same applies to the recognition of others and the integration thereof in our Self. In the discussion on autism we noted what could go wrong and the consequences it has for the person. It is even the case that the recognition of the other as part of our Self is even more important than recognizing many of our own body functions, because our identity is determined to a large degree by the position we have within our social environment. If we are unable to establish contact with our surroundings than we loose a large part of (the control over) our identity. It makes us vulnerable to the 'will to power' which is then always present and a self-perpetuating process. The fear of abuse by others, that forms such an important part of the cause of autistic disorders, is than continuously confirmed. The distrust is at the same time subjective, through the eyes of the distrusting person, as well as objective, when seen from a third person perspective. Our Self is in that case under severe stress and, as we noted in the discussion on automatism and control, it is very hard to create a complete and successful personality that does justice to who you can be in such a situation. Social exclusion from a for the person relevant group is the worst thing that can happen to a person. It is therefore necessary to make compromises, which means that it is not possible to be completely independent. When a person doesn't want to make compromises and is determined to enforce his own will, than cooperation becomes impossible. In that event you don't compromise with other people, but you compromise life because it will limit your possibilities. Eventually it is best to compromise with people who are your friends and have your best interests at heart. People are only complete when they are part of a valuable environment, i.e. if they are accepted by others. In the previous pages we noted that recognition is impossible via the ratio, but that it is only possible through emotions. We will therefore never be able to construct a complete Self if we choose solely for expertise and rational cooperation. Instead we need to do this via identification with others and to open up to them; i.e. through feelings and emotions. Because people have innate structures, like mirror neurons, that are directed at contact and identification with others a full person can never be an atomised individual who has no contact with others. There will always be a need for recognition. This need can be oppressed but that doesn't make it less essential for success in life. The Self is not limited to the atomised individual but stretches out to encompass everything with which people identify with. People are thus by nature directed outward.

The personality characteristics as described by the *Big Five* are partly innate. People have varying degrees of these characteristics. This is partly due to innate abilities but the influence of the environment is also very important. The fact that some characteristics are very important for personal success opens up the possibility for abuse and oppression. It is for example very difficult to be extravert and open in an environment where envy and resentment are abound, while they are very important in creating a successful career and life. When striving for freedom and success we have to make sure that we cultivate those personality traits that best guarantee our success. This is only possible in an environment which is positively inclined towards our Self and does not pose a threat but is a reinforcement. Only in a group are we able to strengthen ourselves mentally and create a strong character. Every strategy that is directed at trying to create a strong character by solely focussing on individual study and meditation will ultimately fail. Also the study of the principles on which the mind works and thereby getting a greater insight can only be a tool, because life can't be learned from a book but only by living, just like riding a bike can't be learned from a book but only by cycling.

We have seen that the Self consists of innate elements like the awareness of our body in the somatosensory cortex, mirror neurons and personality traits. The role of the environment as well as the learning process to use and adapt these elements is also very important in describing the Self. Is this enough to describe the Self or is there more? Is the Self something like the sole? The historical western vision of people consists of a person as having a body and a sole. The sole would ascend to heaven or hell after the death of the body. In many instances people see the essence of the Self as a list of personality traits and memories of previous events. Besides this, many people assume that there must be something more than just these characteristics that determine the essence of who we are. Although science still doesn't know everything about the brain and our body, there is enough information available to state what the Self is not. The Self, that what makes the person who he is instead of someone else, is not an 'essence' that is located somewhere underneath the personal characteristics and memories and other elements of the Self. What defines a person are his specific characteristics. This is similar to a bicycle. Do you still have a bicycle when you remove the wheels, the frame, the saddle, the lights, the gears etcetera? No, the bike consists of these elements and if you remove them you are not left with the essence of the bicycle, but are left with nothing. This also applies to people. A person *is* his characteristics. Alzheimer clearly shows that the person disappears when the characteristics disappear. What about the idea of the soul transcending the body? The fact that our Self can be part of the Self of other persons in our environment gives us some consolation that we are more than our own body as long as those others recognize us and incorporate them in their identity. In this way it is possible to become a little bit immortal. The continuity of our Self is not just a problem after the body dies but also raises questions during our lifetime. Are we the same person we were twenty years ago? Our body changes continuously and almost all our cells are renewed since we were twenty years younger. On top of that we have learned new things and perhaps even turned our entire character around to deal with the changing environment. Still we assume that there is some form of continuity between then and now even if we are not exactly the same person. What has remained the same are our genes and in the end that is all that matters to guarantee our survival.

In present day society many are searching for their Self whereby we see other people as obstacles to be overcome in order to reach this goal. This implies that others are a limitation to us and our development. The ideal society is in such case a 'society' of only one individual. Unfortunately many people don't take the innate human capabilities into account that have been instrumental in the success of humanity. A search whereby everyone tries to find himself without including others leads to a situation in which no-one recognizes each other because everyone is speaking his own 'language'. In previous pages we noted that a person is not an atomised individual but that he is an integral part of the environment. Our brains are on a neuronal level directed at identification and integration of others in our Self. People are flexible creatures that have populated every corner of the globe by adapting to the environment. This adaptation was done by creating a cultural environment that enables people to live in areas that are hostile without changing people in the process. People have adapted the environment instead of that the environment has adapted people. By searching for yourself by excluding others you deny the essential characteristics that determine what it means to be human, because it is only possible to find yourself when you include others. If there is no identification with others than there will be no opportunity to find yourself. This contradiction is abound in modern society. In previous pages we noted that people are by nature inclined to conform to a group and also that we are directed to identification with others. The fact that we remove ourselves from our natural inclination means that there is something in society that oppresses this need. This 'something' consists mostly of competition for scarce resources in a large scale society in which there is recognition for some and not for others.

The search for ourselves is not purely egocentric but is directed at a search for a small-scale group with a good social position. Individualism is not an end-goal but a means to get a high position within a group. It is of course also possible that people will always be searching for themselves without ever finding it. Always on the road but never reaching the final destination. This would not be bad if the means were already the objective from the start, which is unfortunately not the case. The objective is to find the way of life that makes it possible to become happy and have a meaningful life and in that way support the goal of life, i.e. survival. If you are never able to find yourself you will never truly live or be happy. A miserable life is not the only result of such a failed attempt to find yourself, but it also diminishes the chances of survival. Therefore it is of great importance to not only search for yourself but to actually find it. In order to find yourself you need others, because if you close yourself to others you close yourself off from yourself and thereby creating your own demise.

Control and civilized behaviour

According to the prescriptions of civilized behaviour we need to suppress certain thoughts and behaviours in order not to endanger co-existence and stability in society. In the chapter about the Self we noted the negative aspects of trying to gain control over our thoughts and that it is often self-defeating. Actively suppressing specific thoughts activate these thoughts in the unconscious while at the same time causing the conscious to have additional effort to suppress these thoughts. Taking into account that only a limited amount of thoughts can be present in the conscious mind means that the unconscious takes over other tasks when the conscious is busy suppressing thoughts. These other tasks are then automatically processed. The suppressed thoughts are often used in the automatic interpretation of observed behaviour of others, ourselves and the situation because of the high activation level of the suppressed thoughts. This can lead to a self-image in which the suppressed thoughts fulfil a key role. An aspect that makes it increasingly difficult to suppress unwanted thoughts is the fact that the thoughts grow stronger when they are more frequently and longer oppressed. Suppression is therefore a fight with yourself that can never be won. The feeling of guilt and sin can be the result of this process. As we noted in previous pages this problem would never have been present if people were not forced to suppress these thoughts. Most likely these thoughts would never have come to mind, at least not so often or so strong. Abuse and oppression are not far away.

The elite imposes civilized behaviour upon itself thereby suppressing unwanted behaviour and thoughts whereby they consciously decide what is unwanted and what is not. This process of suppression takes cognitive effort which means that there is less room for other thoughts. Although the suppressed thoughts attain a higher activation in the unconscious and thus increase the chances that they are activated it is not the case that when the conscious suppression falls away that these suppressed thoughts immediately surface. In the discussion on habitual behaviour we noted that behaviour and thoughts that are often repeated become automated. To a certain extent this also applies to suppression of unwanted thoughts. It is therefore partly possible to automatically suppress these thoughts in our unconscious even if these thoughts have a higher activation in the unconscious. Learning civilized behaviour in this way takes great effort and is never perfect. The suppression of unwanted thoughts will always require a, limited, amount of cognitive resources. People with a good social position have the luxury to reserve part of their cognitive resources in order to maintain this civilized behaviour. Even they will fall victim to uncivilization (uncivilized behaviour) when they are confronted with a situation in which they have no possibilities to suppress their thoughts. This is due to the fact that suppression can never become fully automatic. An important element in cultivating uncivilized behaviour is related to what Freud called the defensive projection. According to this theory we project thoughts that we deny in ourselves upon others. As we noted in the discussion on conformity there is a strong and innate tendency to conform to the group. People want to belong to a group and social exclusion from a relevant group is probably the worst thing that can happen to a person. This is also true for all those who are not part of the elite but who do want to belong to it. This makes them susceptible to the opinion of the elite. People adapt to others and have the tendency to behave in a way that others see them. The elite use defensive projection to project the thoughts that they deny in themselves onto weaker others. The socially weaker people will then start to behave according to the thoughts and ideas that the elite deny in themselves. People then become uncivilized because the civilized elite use their suppressed thoughts in their interpretation of the behaviour of others. These others will subsequently interpret this as being true and they will see themselves like the elite want them to be. A related aspect is the principle of priming. Hereby a schema or characteristic is activated by a prime, a stimulus, making the person use that particular schema in the interpretation of the observed behaviour of others, themselves and the situation. In this way the elite is able to prime others to see themselves as uncivilized. The socially weaker people therefore have thoughts obtruded upon them causing them to interpret their world on the basis of thoughts that the elite marked uncivilized.

A new form of exclusion

During the age of colonialism much of the world was controlled by the West. In this global system Europeans ruled over Africans and Asians in the assumption that it was the natural order of things. When a clearly distinct ethnic group rules over a different one then both groups often see it as originating from innate capabilities whereby ethnicity is directly linked to societal success. This chapter however deals with a society which is not clearly demarcated by ethnicity but where an elite uses psychological tactics to rule over the people who are in every respect similar to them.

For centuries most societies were static communities whereby the life and career of most people was determined at birth. For example, a child of a shoemaker would most likely become a shoemaker himself. This also meant that there was little room for social mobility. Consequently, most societies had a nobility that ruled over the common people whereby both formed a closed system with the nobles competing with the nobles and the common people with each other. Personal abilities were therefore less relevant than who you were by birth. This changed in the late middle ages when society began to diversify and (international) trade created a more dynamic and open society. Ordinary people could subsequently earn important positions on the basis of merit instead of upbringing. This caused the rule of the nobility to become less self-evident.

The large number of privileges that the ruling nobility enjoyed was not something they would simply relinquish voluntarily now that the common people had access to top positions in society. The elite looked and found a way to give their 'natural self-evident' reign a new impulse, not through nature but through culture. The elite is superior to the common people – not in descent, but in culture or through 'civilization'. The elite is civilized and the others are uncivilized, creating a legitimate reason to distance themselves from the common people and to legitimize oppression, although oppression is ironically also considered uncivilized when rated according to the rules of civilization.

This so-called 'civilized behaviour' or 'civilization' consists of 'good manners' and 'good taste' which consequently makes the bearer of it a better person. The evolution of good manners can be studied by looking into etiquette books and prescriptions on how people should dress, how to care for their body, how to perform a conversation and how others should be addressed. On the basis of these historical documents a pattern emerges of an advancing civilization in Europe whereby the elite become ever more civilized. The elite acted more and more according to the prescribed behavioural patterns which were seen as the only correct behaviour for the elite and which became associated with the legitimacy to rule. For example we notice that the emotions are increasingly controlled, that self-control increases and that interrelations become more formal, detached and standardized. A much heard argument to claim these behaviours to be civilized is that it leaves other people their freedom and dignity and thereby fosters peaceful coexistence. This sounds very noble and civilized and worthy of a ruler. Unfortunately reality is often less beautiful than the propaganda of the elite make it appear.

In previous chapters we noted that the display of emotions is necessary to read other people's minds and to recognize others as equal partners and as part of our Self. We also noted the reasons and pitfalls of self-control. From this we can conclude that these behaviours don't contribute to peaceful coexistence but that they actually undermine the community and strive towards exclusion and oppression of the other. A society based on these civilized values can be characterized as a society which is strongly focused on abusing others and a will to power. Such an environment causes people to display all the characteristics of autism. The result is that people will be trapped in their own world whereby there is no ability for good interaction with others. People are by nature social creatures who can only function properly and become who they can be in interaction with others. The loss of social stimuli can quickly and easily lead to a serious depression that endangers people's survival and future.

The elite might have implemented civilization upon themselves in order to distinguish themselves from the common people but at the same time they separated themselves from the rest of the elite and the world. Many formal manners are therefore prescribed on how to react to certain events and what emotions to feel in order to be able to cooperate and to show other people what your intentions are. People need to learn these forms of behaviour because they are not natural. It is also important to note that we can only recognize the other by simulation of the others' emotions in our brain. It does not work through rational analyses as we noted previously. The recognition of the other works according to the simulation theory and not the cognitive theory. In case the elite were able to completely control their emotions than there would be no opportunity to establish contact with others who are also part of the elite which would prevent them from becoming and remaining an elite. The elite is therefore not able to hide its emotions completely and uses most of the learned civilized behaviour to form a community that sits on top of the population.

Civilization therefore causes people to suppress their natural inclination for positive interrelations and recognition of others in order to survive in a hostile environment where everyone is a potential enemy. Oppressing your emotions makes it difficult for other people to know what you are thinking and thus protects against possible abuse but at the same time decreases the possibility to recognize the other. It dehumanizes others whereby we don't allow the other to become part of our Self. As we will see in discussing the ethics of morality in the next chapter there is no morality outside the Self which makes competition a lot easier because emotions don't come in the way. Unfortunately it also undermines cooperation and causes anti-social and violent behaviour. This also shows that uncivilization is not simply imposed upon the uncivilized people but that the elite has also imposed uncivilization upon themselves. Beneath the civilization that the elite has imposed upon itself there lies uncivilization which was not there before the civilization was imposed. It is therefore not easy to remove civilization because it will reveal uncivilization. Only when everyone in a community throws off civilization and uncivilization is there the opportunity to prevent an escalation of conflict. Removing the system of civilization-uncivilization will make the natural state of people visible which is peace loving against all those with whom there is identification.

What are the consequences of 'civilization' for the common people who have been uncivilized? The key to oppression of the common people lies in the manipulation of their will. Over the centuries the elite became ever more civilized and distant from the population. It was however not the case that the common people stuck to their values as they existed before the elite started their civilization project. With the imposition of civilization by the elite, at the same time uncivilization was imposed on the rest of society. The elite did not just civilize itself but at the same time uncivilized the rest, which is in itself uncivilized. The civilization of the elite was not objectively superior to the manners that existed before. The argument however is that civilization is necessary to survive in a large, complex and open society without harming the other. The old manners are in this line of thinking inadequate and would result in a hostile society without mutual respect and where people would kill each other if they had the chance. This would lead to chaos and barbarism. The civilization of the elite on the other hand prevents this barbaric events from happening. This noble deed of the elite extends itself to oppressing the barbaric behaviour that is still present in the common people. The oppression of the people is in this line of thinking therefore a necessity to keep society intact and protect the people against themselves.

The problem with this line of reasoning is that uncivilization did not exist before civilization was imposed. Uncivilization is a product of the civilization of the elite who by means of psychological manipulations imposes uncivilized behaviour upon the common people. This uncivilization is vulgar, aggressive and anti-intellectualistic which are coincidentally all characteristics which make it more difficult for people to organise and develop themselves. Uncivilization is therefore harmful for future success. It is therefore important to ask why people become uncivilized when the objective of life is survival and uncivilization actively undermines it. The reason for the existence of uncivilization is that the elite has imposed it through psychological manipulations. As we noted in the discussion on consciousness and the will, having a free will is not a question of a onetime decision but a continuous process of thoughts which are partly automatic and circumvent our consciousness and are heavily influenced by the environment. If we wish to protect ourselves from manipulation of our will to desire something that is not in our best interest than we should be aware of the undermining situation. Through reflection and cooperation with others it is then necessary to create an environment that favours our evolutionary success, provides us a free will and eliminates the processes of civilization and uncivilization.

Finally, we look at the abstract moral dimension of civilization-uncivilization. When we judge uncivilization based on the criteria of the values of civilization than the result will be that uncivilization is uncivilized. It is of course also the fact that the elite always determines the moral values of the terminology, but if we judge civilization with the criteria of this same civilization then we also arrive at uncivilization because civilization decreases the ability to cooperate and makes others to become uncivilized. The fact that judging civilization through the values of this same civilization always results in uncivilization, meaning that both civilization and uncivilization are uncivilized, leads to the conclusion that it is not these moral criteria which are important but that there is another hidden morality at work. This morality is to be found in the exclusion and oppression of others. Civilization is therefore a will to power of the elite by trying to control the will of others. The desires of the common people are then objectively speaking bad for them but benefit the elite.

It is furthermore interesting to note that civilization has made society more uncivilized than if there were no call for civilization. Both the elite and the common people are uncivilized according to their own criteria while they were both *civilized* before the rise of civilization. We noted previously that the state of nature of people does not include undermining others or lying and cheating, but that there is a strong tendency to conform and cooperate. These values would dominate life if it were not for the fact that civilization makes everyone uncivilized.

The open society

An open society offers the less endowed more opportunities for social chances and possible rise in status, but it also offers more chances for social decline and exclusion. The continuing differentiation and increasing complexity of society don't automatically mean that society becomes truly open for everyone, in the sense that everyone has access to every position in society. There are numerous barriers that make it difficult for people from a more vulnerable background to become successful. A lack of self-confidence and limited knowledge about the possibilities that society has to offer are very important factors in limiting the chances of those who are not part of the elite. The lack of knowledge of civilized behaviour is also important in this, where this knowledge is not theoretical knowledge but the ability to internalise and control the cultural etiquette of the elite. This control should be seen as habitual behaviour and is the result of practice. It is hereby of course necessary to be in the situation where the behaviour can be learned. This is a form of the chicken and the egg problem – what existed first? A complex, differentiated society is not by definition an open society because it is possible to divide groups in various classes in which every class has its own status and job without the possibility to choose to become part of another group. For many centuries this was everyday reality and up into the 19th century people were limited in their social development. The rise of democratisation and nationalisation meant an increase in equality and the barriers between groups declined.

Nationalism is an ideology that tries to bind the population to the political unit (the state) in such a way that the people, or the nation, coalesces with the state; i.e. the nation-state. The individual persons who are living in a certain area are than nationalized in order to feel part of 'the people' that in its turn is represented in the state. This is the elementary form of self-determination of a people. Every modern state nationalizes its population because if it didn't it would not get enough support to govern effectively. The population has to accept the authority and legitimacy of the state to govern. This only happens if people truly believe that the state represents the people and its individuals. From this assumption we can also conclude that nationalism provides no room for an elite to close itself off from ordinary citizens. Nationalism is therefore the most important ideology to fight uncivilization and provides the socially marginalised people equal access to all positions in society. Nationalism thereby creates an open society for those who have been excluded by the elite. Furthermore, nationalism always falls back on a particular culture with which people identify. The objective of nationalism is therefore to have all members of the nation to share one culture. All European countries did this by standardising the language, education, justice and media. In this way the socially marginalised could no longer be excluded from social positions by not having the right cultural background because everyone ideally has the same background and identity. During the process of nationalisation people are taught to behave in a certain way towards each other and the government. This indoctrination happens through education, the media, legal systems and other societal processes. A crucial objective in this is to turn persons into citizens who together form society and support each other. Another characteristic of nationalism is the fact that it is a continuous process that is never completed; there is no end point. The negative association with nationalism is based on the way in which it is sometimes implemented, meaning the exclusion and elimination of people and groups who do not belong to the chosen group. Seeing that nationalism wants to turn everyone into one group, an exclusion of people is a choice that can be made or not. In almost all instances persons and groups that fall within the power of the state are nationalized. It is therefore the general rule that only when some groups resist this kind of nationalisation policy that resistance in the form of separatism surfaces. In the event that all people are nationalized the result will be an open society which is also open to the previously marginalized.

Ethics of morality

Our emotions stand at the foundation of our decisions and they heavily influence our perception and interpretations of these decisions. The fact that emotions are at the foundation of our rationality indicates that emotions are rational in the sense that rational decisions are impossible without emotions. The way in which people perceive the world and themselves is in terms of intentions. Everything has an objective and purpose. Furthermore, we attribute moral values to acts and intentions.

People see the world as intentional and filled with values, which therefore shows that it is not a scientific worldview. Nature has no objective, purpose or morality, but only facts. The social world of people is therefore not governed by the laws of physics and nature, but by the laws of culture. These laws are based on our morality; answering the questions of right and wrong. The fact that our morality can't be scientifically grounded means that it can never be absolute. This is opposed to scientific laws like the law of gravity which are absolute and valid everywhere. Despite the relativity of morality there is a remarkable homogeneity when it comes to moral values among human beings. The basic moral values of people in different cultures and at different times are very similar. This is a strong indication that the (formation of) morality is mostly innate. This is in line with the fact that our basic emotions are also innate and can be found in all people no matter where they live and who they are. In light of the fact that our morality is based on our emotions we can expect that our basic morality is also universal. Many studies have shown that morality has strong biological links and is innate. It is even the case that our morality is located in the older parts of the brain and that all mammals have a form of morality.

It is the emotions that determine if something is good or bad and without those emotions it will be impossible for us to determine what the right choice is. Morality is however not located in any specific location but is distributed throughout the brain like most other brain processes. Just like all other characteristics of people morality is also the product of evolution. This is despite the fact that evolution can only provide a 'negative justification', i.e. limiting conditions. Morality is than a product of evolution and is based on biological brain processes. It is however not the source for the justification of our morality. The justification of morality is the product of our social environment. Morality is strongly connected with one's own interests whereby this has to be seen from the perspective of the Self as elementary unit; Self-interest. The social world roughly has two types of environments. One being the Self and the second being the Other. The Self is the social environment with which people identify. The Other consists of the outsider. Morality can therefore best be seen as dualistic in which what is good for one's own group can be bad for another group and vice versa. The killing of a person who belongs to the *in-group* is therefore considered murder and a mortal sin, which can have major consequences for our conscience. Killing a person in another group is not necessarily seen as a crime. The latter is in fact not part of morality at all, because the Other is not seen as equally human, but as an object.

The justification of morality finds its origin in (the survival of) one's own group or more accurately in the (survival of the) Self.

People can be manipulated to believe that something is in their best interests while in reality going against their interests. An example is the manipulation of the will of the people to believe that the elite is part of the Self of the average citizen, while in reality this is not the case. On the contrary, in many cases the elite considers the 'ordinary people' as the Others who are less human and therefore don't belong to the group; i.e. the Self of the elite. Morality is based in the Self-interest and is the result of evolutionary processes to guarantee survival by safeguarding against threats from the outside world. Therefore we can conclude that everyone and everything with which there is no identification will not be considered fully human or part of the Self. The primary emotions clearly show this distinction. Fear, anger and disgust are examples of primary emotions directed at preventing and undoing threats that originate from the outside world. Love, friendship, joy and happiness are emotions directed at including equals who then become part of the Self. In order to survive in a dangerous world it is crucial to know when to make this distinction. When we are in a competitive environment we need to see the competitors as the Other in order to protect ourselves and be able to survive. Especially when confronted with a zero-sum competition it is essential to dehumanize the other in order to prevent being destroyed. The fact that human morality is structured in this way means that we have to arrange society based on these characteristics. If we were to ignore the basic make-up of humanity we would be creating an immoral society that will eventually collapse under its own contradictions.

The fact that morality is based on innate human structures means that it is not absolute in the sense of a physical law like gravity, but it also means that it is at the same time not relative. Morality is absolute in the sense that people are unable to choose another morality than the one that is innate. This also means that there is no absolute free will to perform acts which are immoral. For example it is not possible to kill a person with whom there is identification without getting a guilty conscience. Human morality is therefore absolute in the sense that there are innate biological structures that determine what we consider to be right or wrong without the ability for us to change it. This moral heritage will determine our perception of right and wrong, good and evil as long as we are human. At times this may appear contradictory to everyday reality in which crime, corruption and immoral behaviour are frequent and abundant. This is however not the case. For instance a small part of crime is committed by people with serious mental and moral disabilities. Secondly, most corruption takes place because the culprits don't identify with the people they cheat. Furthermore, a lot of crime is rationalized by criminals who place the blame with the victim, the situation or society. This rationalization also shows that most criminals have similar moral standards as the rest of the population. The innate morality would make it impossible for them to perform the criminal acts if they were unable to re-interpret the situation and place the blame somewhere else. De-humanization is a key factor in this. Because it is impossible to disadvantage or seriously damage someone who is part of our Self, we need to de-humanize them. The innate morality that organizes the cooperation of equals is no longer applicable to the victim when we de-humanize that person, which means that he is placed outside morality. Violence against de-humanized enemies has no consequences for our conscience. It is therefore of great importance to determine if the other person identifies with you or if he sees you as a de-humanized enemy who can be eliminated in the competition for scarce resources. The golden rule to do unto others like you would like them do unto you only applies if this other is in fact part of our Self and is not the Other.

The values of the Enlightenment as well as those of religion are unable to state absolute truths and no moral theory will ever be an absolute truth because nature knows no morality, only facts. Evil therefore doesn't exist in nature and is only a projection. In this chapter it is explained that morality only applies to that with which we identify and that there is no morality outside the Self. Morality is by-and-large innate and the result of millions of years of evolution. The distinction between good and evil is therefore deeply rooted in human nature, while at the same time it is not a physical law. The question than arises why it is so important to have the ability to distinguish between good and evil. In short:: Evil is the threat to the Self. Everything that is considered a threat to the successful survival of the person and everything he identifies with is seen, in varying degrees, as bad and as Evil. Furthermore, this evil also needs to be intentional to be truly considered Evil. Natural disasters are therefore not part of this evil as long as we don't consider it to be caused by some divine entity. Evil is applicable to social issues in which we consider other persons as the greatest threat to our Self. The reason for this is that people primarily live in an environment dominated by other people, as opposed to most other animals who are primarily focused on surviving in the natural environment. People can survive almost anywhere as long as the cultural environment functions properly. The awareness of good and evil helps us to distinguish friends from enemies. Because evil is a projection of what we perceive as a threat to our Self it will be impossible to have an absolute definition of good and evil. For example Nazi-Germany is often seen by the West as the embodiment of evil, but this is mostly due to the fact that they were/are a threat to the dominance of the main Western powers. The destruction of the native population of America and Australia is evaluated completely different from the destruction of the European Jews, while the differences are minimal. The main difference is the evaluation of what is perceived as the biggest threat to the Self of the ruling group.

The mechanism of individual human morality also applies to society as a whole. When judging the arguments of a person it is therefore essential to know if you are within or outside morality; if you are within the persons' Self or outside of it. It determines whether you should focus on friendship and cooperation or that you should see the other as an enemy and be prepared to use violence. If there are indications that you are de-humanized than only one response is correct and that is to also see him as the Other and act appropriately. This is a zero-sum game that can only be won if you treat the other as he treats you and to never back down as we will see with the discussion of game-theory. Of course cooperation is the best way to live peacefully but this is only possible if the other is not bent on your destruction and wants to monopolize all resources.

The principle of "the goal justifies the means" is immoral according to the principles of the Enlightenment Sacrificing others to serve your own ideals is also not legitimate; only self-sacrifice would be legitimate. The principles of the Enlightenment are however not an absolute truth and are even proven false by the theory of evolution. The question whether an action can be considered ethical is not to be found in the principles of the Enlightenment or in human nature, but in the morality of the elite in society. The elite determine to a large degree what the ethical norms within society are. This morality is derived from biological brain processes but the distinction between those to which morality applies and those who are outside of it determines if a policy is ethically good or bad. Policy is good if it guarantees the survival of the elite and is bad if it endangers it. The implications for the rest of the population are irrelevant in determining the ethical nature of this policy. The elite needs (part of) the population in order for them to survive, which gives people important leverage to partially take control. This can be done by seeing that the argumentation used by the elite is false and to then act in a way that the elite is to be considered the enemy that is in competition with the rest of the population.

Previously we noted that morality originates from the Self and not from nature. Something similar applies to rationality. It too originates from the Self and doesn't originate from the atomized individual. It is therefore a major mistake to see society as a collection of rationally thinking individuals, because rationality originates from the Self and not the individual. An important indication that rationality originates from the Self and not the individual, comes from experimental economy and is called 'the ultimatum game'. It is often used as an example of the lack of rational behaviour among people in that they act irrational and go against their own interests. The ultimatum game goes as follows: There is an amount of ten Euro. The game is played by two players in which one divides the money and the other can accept or refuse the offer. When he refuses the money both players get nothing. A rational player who thinks only of his own interests will always accept the offer no matter the amount offered. Even if he would get only two Euro, this would be better than nothing. In reality virtually everyone rejects a 80/20 division. The reason for this is that unjust divisions are not accepted and that people will even give up their own success and profit to punish the other. It might appear irrational to give up your own profit to punish the other. The reason why it would appear irrational is because many consider the individual to be the unit of rationality when in fact it is the Self that is the origin of rationality. The Self stretches out from the individual and encompasses the social environment with which a person identifies. Furthermore, people assume that people with which they identify are good (i.e. have the best interest of the Self in mind). The rationality in the ultimatum game is not to be found in the individual but in the Self that also includes the player who makes the offer. The process of distributing the money can therefore be seen as a morally just environment in which it is not allowed to harm the other person who is part of the Self. The feeling of indignation in cases when we are confronted with unfair treatment like in the ultimatum game is an innate human characteristic and enables us to make sure that the other person remains part of our Self so cooperation remains possible. Experiments with the ultimatum game in which the giver and receiver each belong to a separate group where there is little or no identification with each other shows that greater injustice is accepted and harsher punishments are given. The separation between our Self and the Other resurface here again. We de-humanize the other in order for us to win a zero-sum competition. The previous example still had some form of mutual identification and a desire to cooperate, but an escalation of unfair distribution will completely rule out cooperation. When the feeling of indignation with an unfair distribution disappears there is also no desire to punish the other person. Instead of punishment people will only look at getting as much as possible for themselves and cooperation is made impossible. It also means the destruction of the community. Cooperation becomes impossible and society collapses when people are in a life-or-death competition. When the emotion of moral indignation disappears in the case that other people take more than their fair share, identification with others disappears and with it the basis of society. This usually does not happen in a small scale setting but in a modern society structural injustices can continue to exist for a long time which can undermine society. The enormous salaries that bankers give themselves, even if they perform very poorly, are a good example of such a structural injustice. It is therefore crucial for the existence of a modern society that great injustices are dealt with. When injustice is legitimated as being a normal part of a good society than it is also no longer accepted to feel indignation. 'Unfortunately', indignation is a human reaction to injustice and the only way left to function in such an environment is to de-humanize the other and go on a selfish journey to steal as much money as possible. Eventually society, which is necessary to have prosperity, will collapse. There is no unfair competition in a zero-sum game because morality has vanished from the environment. The terms fair and unfair are not applicable in an a-moral environment and all that is left is a competition to the death of one or all. A zero sum competition in which one gets everything and the other is left with nothing is therefore vacuum of values and can't be called fair or unfair. Every reaction is than ethically interchangeable, because morality is irrelevant in such a situation. Eventually only survival remains real and in a zero-sum environment this by definition means the destruction of the other. This can of course lead to great violations of human rights, but even they are in such a situation irrelevant, because human rights are based on morality and not on physical science. We therefore have to take every effort to prevent society becoming so unfair that morality disappears and that even the term unfair is no longer applicable.

Evolution as a description and explanation of life

One of the most important discoveries of the 19th century is the insight into the workings of evolution as formulated by Charles Darwin in 1859. According to Darwin's theory of evolution the diversity and complexity of life is the result of natural selection caused by natural circumstances in which the organisms who are best adapted to their environment survive while the rest dies out. An important element in this is the necessity for variation, whereby the organisms that have characteristics that give them a competitive advantage over others, will survive and subsequently pass these characteristics on to the next generation. Since 1859 the theory of evolution has been expanded with new insights in genetics and molecular biology while the theory itself has stood the test of time. For example, Charles Darwin was unaware of the work of Gregor Mendel who was working on heredity. Darwin thought that characteristics of the parents were mixed in their offspring although genetics clearly shows this not to be the case. The idea that the survival of the individual is the most important factor in the theory of evolution has also been disproven. We now know that evolution is not about the survival of the individual or the group, but that the focus lies on the reproduction of genetic material; from *'survival of the fittest'* to *'inclusive fitness'*. The latter also explains the presence of altruistic behaviour which can't be explained with Darwin's theory of evolution. Helping others when there appears to be no self-interest is called altruism. When we look at evolution from the perspective of individual survival than altruism is always irrational because it only helps the other to survive at the expense of oneself. When we look at evolution on the level of the genetic material than it is actually rational to help others under certain conditions, even if this comes at the expense of personal survival. Children for example inherit fifty percent of their genetic material from each parent, while cousins and other relatives also share part of our genes. It will therefore be good for the survival of our genes to help those closest related to us. The support can be increasingly greater with closer kinship. These improved insights into evolution can offer us a better picture of the influence that nature has on the social position and organization of man-kind in the world.

Social Darwinism has a negative connotation for many because it is associated with eugenics and was used to legitimize social inequality. These are some of the most important reasons why many reject the theory of evolution as a guiding principle in the design of a universal ethical code. Unfortunately people tend to forget that social Darwinism is only an interpretation of the theory of evolution and that politics doesn't get its values from evolution but that it uses Darwin's theory as a means to give other political ideals scientific credibility. Misuse like this doesn't mean that the theory of evolution can be ignored when trying to understand and explain social interaction. Firstly it is important to note that the theory of evolution is not an immoral theory but that it is an a-moral theory. The theory of evolution is a descriptive explanation of how the world works and is not a prescription of how the world should be organized. Although the theory of evolution doesn't know morality of itself it is still necessary that every moral theory is grounded in evolution or else we would get a theory that is detached from reality. Ignoring the principles of evolution would than be immoral because it would harm society which could have been prevented. Therefore evolution in a roundabout way is also a justification of the right life.

Much of the debate on integration and emancipation of minorities assumes an incorrect idea of the theory of evolution. Evolution works on the basis of the principle that organisms that are best adapted to current circumstances will survive. The underlying thought in much of the integration- and emancipation debate assumes that evolution is based on adaptation. This is similar to the theory of evolution that was dominant in the first half of the 19th century and had its main proponent in the person of Lamarck. According to Lamarck the long neck of the Giraffe was the result of stretching the neck by continuous generations of Giraffes. In human terms this can be compared with a man who is into bodybuilding after which his children will later also become muscular. This is of course incorrect and Charles Darwin showed that acquired characteristics are not inherited. Instead, evolution works on the basis of selecting those varieties that are most successful. When we look at the example of the Giraffe, we can see that there were Giraffes with long necks and with short necks. The long necked Giraffes had a greater chance of survival and had more offspring compared to the short necked Giraffes, which meant that the neck of Giraffes became longer over time. When we transpose this proven scientific theory to the ideology of equality as proposed by the Enlightenment than we see that the latter is incorrect. These ideals don't correspond to reality and the state of nature of humanity. In this way we create a society that conflicts with humanity and humaneness. The consequence of a society that is not made for people but for an abstract ideal is that persons who do not fit within this ideal are filtered out and will die out, as the theory of evolution of Darwin has adequately shown.

How should an ethical theory take the theory of evolution into account? How do we connect an a-moral theory with a moral theory? An ethical theory is a theory which proscribes the right way of life and indicates the morally correct way to deal with the world. According to most Enlightenment philosophers and their successors every ethical theory needs to be based on humanity and should provide for the best and most valuable life, in which 'best' and 'valuable' are defined in terms of success in the abstract philosophical system of Kant and utilitarianism. Because people, like all other biological organisms, function within the limits of the principles of evolution, it is necessary to ground an ethical theory in the theory of evolution. If we were to ignore this reality we would be building a theory without proper foundation, which unfortunately has happened many times. The theory of evolution can be compared with the theory of gravity. When an architect has a vision to build the greatest and grandest building of all time, he can not simply wish away gravity if the laws of gravity would hamper his design possibilities. Who would want to live and work in a building in which the designers did not take the effects of gravity into consideration? Such a building could be safe, but it could just as easily collapse under its own contradictions. The same applies to the design of an ethical theory. When we don't take evolution into consideration when designing an ethical theory than the ethical theory will eventually collapse under its own weight and cause many innocent victims. The denial that evolution stands at the basis of any ethical theory is therefore a denial of reality and is pure stupidity. Wishing away evolution is like wishing away gravity when you jump off a high building; you will not notice that your assumptions are wrong until you hit the ground after which it is too late. It is therefore not a question *if* an ethical theory should be grounded in the theory of evolution, but *how* this can best be done.

In what way can the theory of evolution show us what ethical system is fit or unfit if the theory itself has no morality and can therefore never be a justification for the choice of what is the right life? A description and explanation are not justifications and it is always an error of logic to reason from an *is* to an *ought*. Firstly, we can state that the theory of evolution disproves the theory of Divine inspired morality as well as Kantian ethics and utilitarianism, without the theory of evolution formulating its own ethics. The theory of evolution is therefore especially good at disproving social theories and is unable to establish its own normative system. The latter has been tried on many occasions and is known as social Darwinism. The problem with social Darwinism is that many different and opposing values and arguments can be taken from the theory of evolution and that they eventually proved to be rationalizations of power hungry politicians. An ethics of evolution has therefore remained an illusion. Despite these failures it is nonetheless possible to ground human ethics in the theory of evolution if we assume that the facts and insights into the way the world works can help us to guide our moral instincts to better deal with the world. Although it is always an error in logic to reason from an *is* to an *ought*, it is also the case that an *ought* implies that it is possible. The comparison with the theory of gravity clearly shows this to be the case. The theory of gravity does not say what kind of building the architect has to design, but it does state the conditions that the design has to abide by. It is for example possible for a bird to partially defy gravity and to fly, but this is impossible for people.

Millions of years of natural selection have led to a situation in which birds have adapted to flight. Wings, light bones, feathers and great physical fitness make it possible for birds to fly. People on the other hand do not posses these features and therefore make it impossible for them to fly without aid. The aids that people have developed in order to fly take these human limitations into account. It is therefore not people who fly, but it is aircrafts, helicopters or balloons that fly and create an environment that make it possible for people to fly along. Similarly, social theories should offer an environment that takes the limitations of people into account while at the same time enable them to overcome these limitations, like an aircraft enables people to fly without requiring any changes from people's innate abilities. Social theories should therefore take the limitations of human nature as developed through millennia of evolution into account. Hereby it is also good to realize that morality is not based on any physical law of nature but on an, although innate, social construction and therefore always relative without a direct connection to the factual world. If we therefore design a social system that goes against human nature than we have an immoral theory. When an ethical theory for example states that men and women are equal, and the biological structures would deny this, than we are stuck in a self-constructed social prison that will eventually destroy us because it damages our evolutionary fitness. The theory of evolution can therefore be seen as a *negative justification* that 'proscribes' what an ethical theory should not have instead of what it should have.

Why do we need a moral environment when nature itself is a-moral? We need morality because it enables us to know good from bad so we are able to see the threats to survival that are ever present. Nature might be a-moral, but we see everything that could be a threat to our continued existence as a form of evil. People create a social environment to mediate between nature and ourselves in which we need to survive. Without this social environment people are unable to survive. This also implies that a lack of social rules causes survival to be endangered. In that sense nature can be seen as evil, despite the fact that nature itself is a-moral. Nature is a threat to the survival of people if there is no mediating social environment, which makes nature part of evil, from the perspective of people. Fighting evil is therefore always necessary even though people's innate nature is good; i.e. positively inclined towards all those with whom we identify. In many respects nature has been pushed back with the advancement of human technological development when it comes to morality. When we look at the religions of hunter/gatherers we see that natural forces play a large role in their vision of good and evil. This is mainly due to the fact that the forces of nature play such a major role in the survival of hunter/gatherers. The more technologically advanced a society, the less influence natural forces have on the survival of people. In modern society natural forces are mostly replaced by a man-made and socially constructed environment as the greatest threat to survival. Perhaps technology itself will in the future become the greatest threat and most important source of evil.

The ultimate objective of biological organisms (within their limited existence) that live according to evolutionary principles is simply to survive in the sense of the guarantee of continued existence. An essential part of an ethical theory should therefore be survival. How this should be implemented in an ethical theory is not as straightforward as at first glance might appear. This is due to the complexity of life and the fact that the ultimate survival could even mean that a person looses his life. On top of this is the fact that evolution is shortsighted and that it does not have a long-term strategy. This means that those characteristics survive which guarantee the greatest success at the current moment, while characteristics that are less successful now but could provide a greater success in the future, don't survive. It should therefore be an objective of any ethical theory to enable people to rise above these limitations of evolution and become the ultimate survivor. We have the ability to look ahead and notice the pitfalls and adapt our social environment to a situation that lies ahead. This does not mean that we rise above evolution, but it does mean that we are better able to adapt to the whims of nature and increase our chances of survival. However, history has shown us time and again that the processes of evolution lead to ever more complicated and specialized life-forms, but that there are periodic fallbacks in which the most specialized organisms die out and the 'lower' organisms survive. The extinction of the dinosaurs is a good example of this, as is the extinction of the Mega-fauna of the last ice-age. Those animals that were best adapted to a certain environment and stood on top of the food pyramid died out. It is therefore incorrect to say that evolution means progress. The term progress is not applicable to evolution, because evolution has no purpose or objective. It is for example not an objective of humanity to rise above itself in order to become an übermensch, just as it is not an objective of chimpanzees to rise above themselves and become human. This is rather an expression of self-hate in which we downgrade ourselves which can lead to self-destruction. An important difference between people and other animals is that people live in an environment that has been mostly created by themselves. This means that evolution doesn't stop, but that we can steer the way it applies to us to a certain extent by the choices we make on how to organize society. When doing this we need to prevent society becoming detached from reality, because that would make it difficult to react properly to threats from outside our self-constructed environment. There is inevitably a future, but it is not certain that humanity is part of that future..

Rights and identity

Nature is without values and morality can only be found within the Self. Something similar applies to rights. Rights are not part of nature but are social constructs to enable social interaction to run smoothly. There can therefore never be such a thing as individual rights because rights always refer to possibilities of living within a particular social organization. A plea for rights is therefore always a plea to become part of the Self of others. Rights are therefore never objective, although they find their origin in an innate human morality. The main action in granting rights is then to recognize the other as part of our Self. This also implies that there are no rights in a zero-sum competition, because there is no morality outside the Self. In the event that there is no intend to grant rights to certain persons and groups then the only option left open to them is to look for rights in their own group. It is therefore crucial to create a social-cultural environment in which the rights can be found in the event that these rights are denied by others. It is not diversity but the loss of identity that is opposed by those who exclude others. In a competitive environment a strong and exclusive identity is crucial for survival.

The elite creates an illusion that success in society is due to individual hard labour and that to make distinctions between people is not legitimate although this is the basis of elite rule. This is an incorrect vision of how society works. The West is not rich because they are smarter or work harder but because they cooperated better and excluded others. Failure to recognize this principle leads to a demise of the weak. It is not hard work that liberates people but it is cooperation and sometimes exclusion that sets people free. As we noted in previous chapters people are wholly dependent on their social surroundings for their survival. Manipulation through our unconscious is strongly present in a competitive environment and decreases our chances of success. We therefore need to surround ourselves with positive stimuli in order to become successful and happy. The shortcut to success is then to surround ourselves with a positive social environment.

Even in the era when globalisation claims to have universal human rights it is good to realize that these 'universal rights' only apply to those who are recognized as fully human by the world's powerful. Everyone with whom there is no, or partial, identification will therefore not share in the universality of rights. The war of the 1990's in Bosnia is a good example of people who according to the world's powerful are fully human and therefore deserve protection when they are the victim of mass human rights violations. The situation in Sudan on the other hand was not seen in the same light although the atrocities were at least as bad. Unfortunately, these victims were not considered fully human and therefore the 'crimes' were not real crimes but only events that did not require actions to stop it. A crime implies the existence of a morality, but the victims in Darfur were de-humanized making it not a crime but an event that happens like a force of nature. Something similar also applies to the Holocaust in World War II, which is seen as a grave crime against humanity and is commemorated in most Western countries as something never to happen again. It thereby achieves a mythical form whereby the West was somehow a victim, like the Japanese commemorate the nuclear bombs to claim they were a victim of World War II as well. The horrors of colonialism and slavery are on the other hand not commemorated by the West even though many millions of people perished and several continents were almost wiped out. This unfortunately also shows that the West still holds 'their own people' as centre of absolute morality thereby de-humanizing all others. Human history is full of atrocities, but it is good to realize that they only become a crime when the victims are considered fully human. World War II and colonialism should not simply be seen as warnings against racism but as a warning that it is necessary to protect one's own group and to make sure identification is not lost. When identification disappears so do the rights. In light of the fact that it is the emotions that determine identification, disappearance of emotions in favour of a-moral regulations will lead to the disappearance of morality and to the loss of rights.

Morality of the law

People have free will despite possible manipulation by others and the major role the unconscious plays in decision-making. Due to this free will people are responsible for their actions and should be held accountable, so as not to endanger the survival of the community. We previously noted that it is not the laws of nature that form the foundation of morality but that it is the Self. In light of the fact that justice is an implementation of morality indicates that it also traces its origin in the Self and not in nature.

The law is therefore always a product of the Self and the community that it creates.

The law finds its origin in the morality of the Self and the community which makes it necessary for judges to take the morality of the community into consideration in their judgments. Judges therefore do not *implement* the law but *interpret* it in order to come to a fair and just judgment. The terms fair and just should therefore be seen as everything that does justice to the community whereby the cohesion and survival of the community is confirmed. The rights of the community are therefore more important than the rights of the individual victim or the perpetrator. In a democracy judges interpret the laws that have been created by the democratically elected parliament. When the parliament is representative of the people laws will be created that enable the community to prosper in freedom. In a true democracy there will therefore be an overwhelming influence of the people on the creation and upholding of laws for the community.

Unfortunately, even the most democratic societies often have a large separation between the people and the judiciary as well as between the judiciary and the legislative. This situation is legitimized as being necessary to uphold the independence of judges and the law. It is an integral part in the separation of powers or the *trias politica* which is supposed to make a democracy a 'constitutional democracy'. A constitutional democracy should be able to offer protection against the dictatorship of the majority (=the dictatorship of democracy…?). The idea behind the separation of powers is that the majority has to be protected from itself when they decide to create policy which is harmful to them, as well as to safeguard any minorities from the majority. It is in such a system the task of the elite, which appoints itself as independent arbiter, to impose justice upon the people. In light of the fact that justice is a reflection of the morality of the community means that the 'independence' of the judiciary (from the opinions and wishes of the people) means that it is not the morality of the people that governs but the morality of the elite that controls the courts. What insights do judges have that the democratically elected representatives or the people themselves don't have? Judges base their verdicts on the laws but it is the population that chooses the lawmakers to create laws that create the desired social order. When judges interpret the law in such a way that it does not reflect the wishes of the people then democracy is undermined and a democratic deficit is present.

The great advantage of having a separation between the judicial, executive and legislative powers is that it prevents abuse, not from the people but from the elite. Although politicians claim to represent the people, they often represent mainly themselves. It is therefore a threat to society that the (political) elite identifies only with each other and not with the people and tries to hold on to power in any way it can. This threat is ever present because the main objective of politicians is to gain power. By creating a separation between creating the laws and executing them, a situation is created that the elite is unable to abuse its powers too much. The separation of powers is therefore mainly to make sure that one elite is unable to monopolize all power. Other elites have to be present to prevent one elite monopolizing power whereby these elites create a balance of power. This might be effective in preventing one elite to gain absolute power, but it also prevents the general population from controlling its own destiny and as such it is an enormous democratic deficit. A possible solution could be to have people elect judges as well as politicians. It is no threat to society when the judicial system is democratized. It is however a threat if undemocratic politicians try to influence justice for their own gain.

The judiciary is independent from the legislative but it is not impartial due to the fact that they form an elite by themselves and take the standards of this social group as basis of their morality.

In following chapters we will see that the survival of the people stands at the foundation of democracy. This implies that the law is necessary to safeguard the survival of the people and to keep democracy functioning. It is hereby necessary that the laws are in the best interest of the population and not of those of the elite. This becomes clear when we look at the consequences of a law. A law creates a situation where potential possibilities in the community are transformed to become real possibilities whereby the limits are demarcated. In this way it is possible to punish those who cross these limits and provide the rest the ability to profit from the offered freedoms. If laws favour the elite, or if they are interpreted in such a way as to favour the elite, than the elite gains freedom at the expense of the rest of the population, who are then less free. This limitation on freedom is because a law also excludes other potential possibilities which can now not be realized. A law that favours the elite automatically harms the population and is therefore undemocratic.

When is violence legitimate?

When is the use of violence legitimate? Buddhism for example claims that nonviolence is the perfect ideal while Christianity and Islam both have the principles of holy wars. The values of the Enlightenment might appear to resemble Buddhism but can in fact better be seen as a holy war against everything that presents a different model of society.

In this chapter we will see that justice can only be implemented through the use of violence but that this violence also has to be accepted by its victims to become justice instead of it being injustice. The law is based on violence to enforce regulations that not everyone agrees with (for himself). In light of the fact that modern democracy can not exist without laws indicates that there will always be a form of violence present in society that we accept as legitimate. Nonviolence is anti-social and undermines the community. Violence is necessary to protect the community against free riders and criminals. When these are not punished, society will irrevocably disintegrate. Furthermore, violence is also necessary when you are confronted with an aggressive opponent with whom you are in competition for scarce resources. Nonviolence would be suicide in a zero-sum competition. It is necessary to be a hawk when you are confronted with hawkish behaviour if you wish to survive.

The use of violence is social and altruistic because the person who uses violence sacrifices himself for the community that is under threat. Violence has the tendency to attract violence which indicates that the person who uses violence has a greater chance of becoming a victim of violence himself. When violence is not used in the event that people are oppressed and abused than they are considered as not being fully human whereby their situation is not significant enough to merit the use of violence. In such an event there is no identification with the victims of violence and instead only egoistic self interest is present.

A degree of violence is necessary when you are not part of the ruling elite. As we noted previously human survival is primarily dependent on the social environment and not primarily on the laws of nature. People create a social environment that maximizes their potential success and survival. Elite will try to organize society in such a way that their success is maximized. This always comes at the expense of others because elite can only hold on to their profitable position if they are hierarchically above the rest of society. This causes all those who don't belong to the establishment to be faced with a social environment that disadvantages them in their potential success and survival. A social system is therefore never objectively fair because it is always directed at creating an environment in which a group of people can be as successful as possible which by definition favours the elite. Success in a social environment is therefore not determined by superior objective qualities, but whether the person is better fit according to the rules as they are applicable within the social system. These rules are in favour of the establishment making it impossible for outsiders to be truly successful if they work according to the rules of the system. The only possibility to become successful is to change the system in such a way that it favours your skills and identity. The establishment will strongly protest this and will reject any potential change as being morally bad. In light of the fact that there is no morality outside the Self and people are excluded by the elite means that there is no such thing as morally good or bad. An appeal based on holding a moral high ground is therefore always misleading. A system in which people are not part of the establishment by definition has to be abolished by them because else they will be destroyed by it. The system has to be replaced by a system that favours your qualities and identity. Only if you make the rules will there be a chance of success.

The origin of violence can be traced to the battle for scarce resources whereby it is necessary to use violence against others. This can be considered instrumental violence. Another origin of violence is the response to a feeling of injustice. When a person or whatever he identifies with is done injustice the emotion of rage can develop. This emotion has an action impulse whereby aggression is raised in order to overcome the cause of the injustice. Such counter violence can undo injustice and it can also prevent future aggression from others. Display of violence can scare off potential enemies because they are afraid the violence might hurt them. Fear is a very powerful emotion. A threat can cause us to become afraid which diminishes our capacity to compete and win in society. The best way to overcome fear is through aggression. Aggression therefore prevents potential enemies to display violence, enables us to undo injustice and finally also takes away our fear. Unfortunately violence also has the tendency to attract violence and all parties have to behave like hawks in order not to lose the zero-sum competition. The violence will then escalate until one or both of the parties are destroyed. Such a downward spiral can only be prevented if people acknowledge that violence is not the best solution for a specific situation and instead opt for cooperation. Cooperation is only possible if there is a win-win situation and the other is recognized as part of the Self. In a zero-sum competition an opponent is necessarily dehumanized but in order to cooperate the other must be seen as a fellow human being and therefore as part of the Self. A major difficulty in this is that the person who concedes first will appear weak and can be overrun. A standard resolution of such a problem is to add a third person to the conflict to act as mediator. This is a form of the resolution of the avoidance-avoidance conflict. In an avoidance-avoidance conflict there is a choice between two undesired alternatives whereby the repulsion increases when the alternative gets closer and decreases when the alternative moves further away. The only solution to such a conflict is to add desirable elements to one of the alternatives in order to make it less undesirable.

We previously noted that violence is used against Others and that it is therefore outside morality. Many violent environments are however not completely devoid of recognition of the other as human but in many cases other people are seen as missing essential human characteristics making them less human. In that way there is still a minimum amount of morality present in most violent conflict situations. A minimized morality demands that others are recognized as equal participants in a violent game without recognizing them as fully part of the Self. In such a game there is no legitimacy in complaining about getting hurt because that is the 'morality' of the game that all participants acknowledge as legitimate. Unfortunately, playing this game means that you are excluded from other environments which could offer a better chance of survival. People are therefore a prisoner of a system that damages their overall ability for success and the only way to be successful is to change the system or to leave it for another one.

It is not possible to kill a person with whom you identify because it would cause a feeling of guilt that harms your physical and emotional integrity. Furthermore, it also causes isolation because others will perceive you as a threat and will disassociate themselves from you. We noted previously that there is an innate and uncontrollable urge for recognition. In the event that a person is completely isolated and therefore not receives any recognition this will create a situation whereby people will look for recognition in a situation in which this is highly inappropriate. Looking for recognition in a zero-sum competition is for example suicide. There is also the phenomenon that the urge for recognition makes people to provoke conflict because there is often some recognition in conflict. Isolation and a hostile environment create a will to power whereby it might appear to be individualistic but where in fact people are completely dependent upon the situation.

Taking another person's life is only harmful to our conscience if that person is recognized as fully human. For example in a war it is easy to kill another person as long as that person is dehumanized. An example of this is the Marshall effect whereby many soldiers in World War II at first did not aim directly at the enemy when firing their guns because they did not dehumanize them enough. This is a good example of the good nature of people even if it places their own survival at risk.

The generally accepted competition in our society is also a form of violence whereby some win and others loose. What violence is justified? Do we have free will in displaying any kind of violence? Violence can only be effectively used against persons with whom there is no identification, which provides us an important clue into the rationality and morality of violence. We noted that instrumental violence is used to win scarce resources and provide safety. Violence can therefore be justified if we are in a zero-sum competition because such an environment has no morality. In order for it to be legitimate it is necessary that this zero-sum competition is not created by us but that we are confronted by it. In a zero sum competition no morality is present which means that the goals always justify the means. Violence is also justified in the protection of others with whom we identify. If such a person or group is under threat than it is an act of compassion to use violence to free them from their oppressed position.

The reasons under which many violent actions are approved are often not the real reasons but are smokescreens for underlying motives. Nonetheless, there are enough situations which merit the use of violence. When people let themselves be intimidated and thereby fail to display the necessary violence that the situation demands than people can loose control over their own situation and life's chances. It is than easy to fall into a depression and suffer from learned helplessness as well as loose access to society's means needed to become successful. Related to this is the difference between statistical violence and the sense of insecurity. Many statistics show a decrease in violence while the feeling of insecurity remains high. This discrepancy is often explained away by blaming people for being irrational and ignorant. Such a blame game is a good example of the delusion that the system is correct but that people are inadequate. Statistics don't describe all violence and don't show the impact it has on people. When the situation is 'objectively' (meaning according to statistics) violent but people have the feeling that they can control the impact of that violence through for example counter violence than the feeling of insecurity will be less than when there is no control over the violent situation. It is therefore not just the degree of violence that poses a threat but the feeling that there is no control and that people can be victimized without defense that is the cause of fear. The objective statistics are of course also important because a violent environment has an unconscious influence on our physical condition because of the fact that certain signals are automatically perceived without cognitive processing and subsequently determine our behaviour and perception of the situation.

The way in which we react to violence depends to a large degree on the evaluation of the situation and what society thinks as acceptable. An example of this can be the attitude of the passengers and authorities during the hijacking of planes in the US in 2001. Up till that time it was assumed that hijackers would ask ransom to get attention for their cause. The use of violence was geared towards this scenario. The government did not shoot the planes out of the sky neither did the passengers try to overpower the hijackers because they thought the best thing was to wait for negotiations. Only when people noticed that the planes were being used as weapons this attitude changed. If people had known the result of the hijacking than the counter violence would have been completely different. The hijackers misled the passengers and the government in order not to be confronted with counter violence. Such a manipulation is also present in everyday life whereby everyone will try to mislead their opponents that counter violence would be wrong in order to keep willing victims. A correct interpretation on the use of possible violence is therefore very important. In case another person profits from a conflict situation at your expense than the use of counter violence is always legitimate.

The threat of violence is also violence because the threat implies a warning that life threatening violence will be used when certain rules are broken. For example the mere presence of police, football supporters, criminal gangs and other groups should therefore already be seen as violence.

When it is no longer possible to participate in the public debate than democracy ceases to exist. The worst violence in a democracy is therefore the violence and threat of violence that closes the public domain off from the people. According to the morality in a democratic system it is legitimate and necessary to resist and be violent if the democratic system is in danger. When a political system is only democratic for a certain part of the population and excludes others than it follows that resistance by the excluded group is obligatory. When an elite excludes the population from the public debate democracy is under threat and resistance is called for.

Morality of the state and the democratic process

An important characteristic of a modern and free democratic state is that the public domain should be a-moral. In this way there is room for persons and groups who have differing opinions and ways of life to co-exist. The state should therefore not be ideological, because an ideology would infringe on the individual freedom of its citizens. We noted previously that nature is a-moral, while human co-existence is always normatively organised with distinctions between good and bad. Human co-existence is impossible in an a-moral environment. Furthermore, we noted that it is impossible to obtain values from facts. It is therefore surprising that the idea of an a-moral state is still seriously considered. The state is not a product of nature but is a social construction to help a community of people to live together. From here it follows automatically that the state always has a morality. If the state would not have a morality than people would not know what policy should be implemented because there would be no sense of what is important and what is not. It would therefore be detached from social reality.

The fact that the state always has a morality has major consequences for the way in which we have to look at the public domain. The public domain has a moral basis. It is therefore not the case that the public domain acts like a vacuum or buffer zone which gives people the freedom to have their own beliefs without limiting the others in their beliefs. A public domain which is vacuum of values creates a complete isolation of the individual from every other individual. Taking into account human nature with the Self as elementary building block, this would mean not only an alienation from the other but also an alienation from oneself. If people see 'rationality' as something a-moral and rational-scientific than this rationality does not mean greater freedom but in fact acts like the opposite because people are isolated from a valuable existence in a moral environment.

The reasons for why some people plead for an a-moral democratic state is partly due to the way democracy is defined. In everyday speech democracy is seen as the rule of the people over themselves. Democracy is than opposed to other ways of government whereby only one or a small group rules. The democratic state is thus based on the desires and interests of the people. In political science, democracy is somewhat differently defined than simply the rule of the people, by the people and for the people. According to the most common political theory the essence of democracy is not a specific defined content but it is the procedure to come to a result, a Truth, whereby the democracy in itself has no objective other than the creation of the public domain in order to make the search for Truth possible. This public domain than has to create an environment in which all persons have the ability to participate in the public debate as equals in order to get to the best possible truth together. To this end the public domain should not be based on a morality and should also be devoid of power. The conclusion that follows from this theory is that democratic procedures should be a-moral and without objective. When people decide to justify and legitimate the democratic procedures by formulating an objective for them, then democracy itself is denied and should therefore be seen as an undemocratic act. It is than not the people that rule but it is a certain Truth that rules. A democracy can therefore not be based on a Truth but should instead be undetermined and empty of values. In a democratic society people will be continuously searching for new truths that are constantly being formed in the public domain ensuring that there will never be one Truth that comes to sit at the basis of democracy. In this line of thought it is assumed that any truth can be lost but that being directed at getting to the truth will always remain. This is therefore a Truth (!) of democracy.

Unfortunately there are some crucial errors in this description of democracy. In previous chapters we noted that nature is based on physical laws of nature, but that the human world is always based on values. In light of the fact that democracy is not a physical law of nature but that it is a social form of organisation by people means that democracy can never be devoid of values without it becoming worthless. The idea of freedom for example is essential for the democratic process to function properly and is strongly connected to values and ethics. Freedom is not an object that we own but is a possibility to do something. In order to have freedom we need to have an idea of what the right choice is, meaning that we need to have a sense of good and bad. If we did not know right from wrong than we would not know what to do and our freedom would be an illusion. In order to have freedom you need to have a morality. This implies that there should be a morality within the democratic procedures because else freedom can not exist and therefore democratic debate would not exist either. As we saw in previous chapters morality is for the most part innate and the result of evolutionary selection to maximize survival. The foundation that lies underneath the freedom to do something as well as underneath the democratic procedures that make the search of society for truth possible is than to maximize the survival of the individual and the community. Democracy therefore should be based on an underlying truth and the procedures and process should have a morality.

A second reason why people plead for an a-moral and neutral state is because it is deemed necessary for the co-existence of different ways of life within one political unit without there being an imposition of an ideology upon individuals. This line of thought assumes that people are completely autonomous individuals. Others are than not necessary and are even a limitation to the freedoms of the individual. We noted in previous chapters that this is not the case. People can never be themselves without interaction with and recognition of others. Individualism is therefore not the objective but only a means to get a good social position within a community of significant others. The classic form of liberalism is therefore based on an incorrect image of human nature. The public domain is always full of values that influences everyone in it and defines the identity of the people to a large extent as well. The fact that many deny the morality of the public domain does not mean that the morality somehow doesn't exist. It is more an indication of the great success of indoctrination of the people.

The observation that one normative system is better able to organize society than the other provides the best evidence that it is at that moment in time closest to the best truth. The truth of a social system is always relative and not a scientific and objective truth. The public domain in the West is therefore filled with the values of the Enlightenment and not with the science and rationality that claim the Enlightenment.

Public and private morality

A difference between a public- and private morality is generally accepted to exist. Behaviour in the public domain is than different from that in the private domain because the morality is perceived to be different towards private as opposed to public groups. We noted previously that there is no morality outside the Self meaning that ultimately their can only be one morality. The apparent difference between public- and private morality is explained here.

In modern society we notice two trends in relation to public and private morality. Firstly, there is a trend towards unity of the two in which the entire population is recognised as being part of the same identity and sharing the same rights. If this trend continues there will eventually be only one morality for all, which is that the private morality becomes the public morality as well.

A second trend however works opposed to this trend for unity and goes towards segregation of the population into small clans. In order to understand this phenomenon we need to take human nature into consideration. We noted that people are by nature conformists and that the social environment has a very strong influence on people. This influence is so great that a large part of the Self is outside the physical person. The social unit is not the atomized individual but includes the social environment with which people identify. The fact that our consciousness is in large part circumvented when judging the environment indicates that it is crucial that our direct social environment can be trusted to have our best interest in mind because the unconscious can be directly influenced. We also noted that through priming and accessible constructs a situation can arise whereby we become the slave of our environment in which an elite implements uncivilization upon us. Such potential abuse is in an individualistic society prevented by closing oneself off from the environment causing us to become partly autistic. Although it protects against abuse it also makes us socially handicapped whereby the chances of success diminish. The only possibility to become a complete person when confronted with a hostile environment is to focus on another environment which is positive and has the best interest of the person in mind. This environment of equals can than be considered the bearer of private morality. This private morality is equal, friendly, honest and fair, while the public morality is dangerous and impersonal with a zero-sum competition. The private domain is than the safe house from which people hide from the competition in the public domain. It is obvious that everyone who does not belong to a strong private domain will have a tough and unsuccessful life. It is not only individuals but also society in general which is harmed by a disappearing morality in the public domain.

If everyone retreats from the public domain in order to find morality in the private domain than citizenship disappears and society disintegrates. In order to stop this degenerative process it is necessary to inject the public domain with private morality in order for people to trust each other again. When even the private morality is corrupted and is disappearing then more drastic solutions are proposed. In such an event often a completely new morality is promoted that usually finds its legitimacy in nationalism or religion. It is however not easy to implement one private morality for an entire country without at the same time fundamentally changing the mentality and structure of society. The reason for this is that people retreat from the public domain to escape oppression. If the safety of the private domain disappears and the public domain does not change for the better than survival comes under threat. In a situation whereby we have an inhuman public domain it is therefore important to keep the private domain intact and at the same time strengthen the public morality with values from the private domain. Community values need to be created to bind the various private domains to each other that will eventually merge into one private domain for all, creating a public domain with the private morality. If this is not done society will eventually disintegrate.

A difference between a public- and a private morality indicates that society is in crisis and that potential abuse is the most important element of the public domain. It also indicates that the existence of a group with a different morality for themselves than for the rest of society is a threat to the entire system because it indicates that this group either is oppressed or is the oppressor. If the latter is the case than the rest of society is left with little option than to create a private domain and try to undermine the other's private domain in order to eventually come to one private/public domain.

Debate in the public domain

The way in which we try to convince other people that our opinions on public policy are correct is in a democracy ideally done through debate in the public domain. In order to have such a debate it is necessary to have a certain degree of freedom of expression. A debate between people who share the same opinions is not a debate but a statement. We assume that a debate leads to one side being won over to the arguments of the other side. A problem is that a debate is by definition a competition and a conflict between people and/or groups. In a zero-sum competition it is imperative to hold on to one's own views and attack the other even if their ideas might be good as well. If we would not do this we would be overrun. Debate therefore enables people to speak but does not help them to be heard. In order to convince the other of the merits of your arguments there is a need for more than debate. Debate creates conflict and separation whereby consensus and mutual identification are needed to come to an adequate solution to the problems that a society faces

Freedom of expression is necessary to enable people to voice their opinions. The more people are able to express themselves the better the chances are that the best choices are made available. The limits society places on freedom of expression are the result of what that society sees as the morally just environment and are thereby by definition relative. This relativity means that it is very hard to judge other time periods because of the different norms and values of the time. What a society regards as acceptable freedom of expression is everything which enables society to move forward in its quest for the best truth that guarantees survival. This means that it is by definition relative because nature has no concept of progress in the moral sense. Limiting freedom of expression is therefore due to perceived threats to (the elite of) society.

The idea that we reap what we sow is often used as an argument to keep unwanted opinions out of the public domain. It is true that opinions are able to spread because they are present in the public domain, but it is not the case that every opinion of every person will always dominate the public domain. On the contrary, most opinions are brushed aside as irrelevant or unwanted by the majority of the population. Opinions will quickly disappear if there is no fertile ground for them within the public domain. It is rare that an opinion creates its own fertile ground from scratch. There are for example always people who call for a revolution but this is almost always brushed aside as the ravings of the village idiot. In those cases that revolution really breaks out it is almost always the case that there was already massive support for the idea but that forces in society prevented these opinions from surfacing. The person who calls for a revolution is almost never solely responsible for an actual revolution but is primarily a medium that makes oppressed feelings and opinions visible and provides solutions for them.

A country or people which is under threat will often implement large limitations to their freedom of expression because they fear unity might disappear and with it society itself if conflict is allowed to roam free. This is a natural reaction but also makes it increasingly difficult to look for possibilities to escape from the oppressed situation. Strengthening of the public domain by increasing identification with each other is than the only option to keep the public domain free.

The outcome of a debate in the public domain clearly shows that this domain is full of values. A debate centres around the fact that other people can be convinced by arguments given by the opposite side. This can never be devoid of values because the objective is to convince others of a certain idea. Such a choice depends on the question if we value one argument over the other. As noted previously nature has no objective or values and only consists of facts and events. When we only take the facts into account there will not be a possibility to decide which facts are more important than others and why. This means that the democratic process as well as the outcome is filled with values. The power in a democracy has therefore strong links with the moral values that dominate in society.

Power is in a democracy usually more widespread than in a dictatorship. This doesn't mean that everyone has equal power. Nonetheless the power of the elite in a democracy is different than that of a dictator in a dictatorship. The power of the elite is mostly given to them by the people they represent. This doesn't mean that the population has simply handed the power over to the elite. Representatives get their power by convincing the population that they are better able to deal with their interests. This is a continuous interaction between the arguments of the representatives and the interests of the population. Power is in an idealised democracy not clustered with the political elite but present everywhere. The fact that acquiring power is the main objective of politicians and that they have to do this in the public domain means that the debate in the public domain is not directed at objectively searching for the truth. Participants in the debate will try to win at any cost. Although power is distributed over large parts of society yet so is the abuse of power and the threats of violence.

A debate eventually leads to a truth that subsequently has to be implemented by government. Some see this truth as a consensus that was reached because everyone acknowledges that it is indeed the best choice. Unfortunately, this is only partly correct. Although it is the case that democratic government policy is supported by a large part of the population it is very rare that this support is universal. When the entire population would be in agreement of a certain decision than government would not have to implement policy to enforce it because everyone would do it anyway. This rarely happens. Despite this lack of consensus on the correctness of decisions there does exist consensus about the way in which the decisions have been made. There is therefore a consensus about the correctness of the process with which a decision is reached even if not all agree on the outcome of that process. We agree to disagree.

The law is based on violence to enforce regulations that not everyone agrees with (for himself). In order for the law to be considered legitimate the victims of violence need to agree with this violence. If this was not the case we would not have justice but instead have war. The fact that the public domain is completely filled with power and the ever present competition for more power means that dishonesty is more the rule than the exception. Democratic processes are often portrayed as fair and transparent, which they often are not. People with more power have the tendency and ability to manipulate the situation in order for them to get the benefits of the system. It is thereby important that the image of honesty remains intact in order not to loose the support of the population for the workings of the democratic process. If the support of the people for the democratic process disappears so does the consensus and the public domain itself. We noted previously that the feeling of justice is very strong and even takes precedence over our own best interests. Dishonesty like corruption should be dealt with in order for people to keep faith in the democratic institutions. If it continues to be unpunished democracy itself will eventually collapse.

Political parties and the demarcation of the public domain

Modern democracy is dominated by political parties with various ideologies. Socialism, liberalism and conservatism are currently the main ideologies. These ideologies form the foundation from which political parties search for a truth in and for society. We noted previously that some claim that democracy should be without values or foundation because if there would be a foundation of democracy it would be the ideology that governs and not the people. Political parties on the other hand are based on a political ideology that shapes the forming of ideas for the best policy and therefore it is not the people but the ideology that governs these political parties. We also noted that there is always an underlying value in a democracy, which is based in the survival of the group. Liberalism, socialism and all other ideologies and religions are essentially unproven, incomplete and non-scientific ethical systems who each claim to offer the best way to guarantee survival.

We noted previously that many claim that the democratic process should be devoid of values and morality in order to be truly democratic. Political parties on the other hand are based on an ideology from which they perceive society. Proponents who claim that democracy should be without morality and that political parties are necessary for democracy to function usually pretend that parties are simply participants in the debate like every other person or group. In that way it is claimed that democracy itself is without ideology while there is the possibility to freely choose one or more of the ideologies that political parties represent. Unfortunately this reasoning is incorrect because the environment in which political parties have to operate is demarcated by the 'morally just environment'. It is for example not allowed for a political party to have 'anti-democratic' principles. Those parties are excluded from the public domain and debate and are usually outlawed. The idea that the debate is completely free and open to all people and opinions is therefore incorrect. The conditions to participate in the debate are determined by the degree to which these ideas are within the limits of the morally just environment. In light of the fact that these limits are determined by the dominant powers in the public domain means that the debate is tilted in their favour. Ideas which might provide a better solution for problems in society but that are damaging to the elite therefore rarely enter the public domain or only marginally. The problems however do not disappear and only increase their potential harm to all those who are not part of the elite.

Western democracy is based on the values of the Enlightenment which means that only ideas and activities approved by it are allowed to enter the public domain. It is therefore the Enlightenment that governs and not the people. The values of the Enlightenment, like all values, are not absolute but are nonetheless implemented as though they were absolute. Much policy is implemented that although good from the perspective of the values of the Enlightenment is not good for the best survival of a large part of the population. Where people warn against a possible take-over of democracy by a Truth that could eventually lead to a dictatorship we are faced with the reality that this already is the case for all of Western democracy. The correct warning that a wrong truth can lead to the demise of the people is ignored and surrounded by a taboo.

Political parties are not simply powerful players in the public domain but are actually responsible for the creation of much of this domain. It is for example the debate within political parties that determines a large part of the Truth. This debate is the exclusive domain of politicians from the particular parties. The debate in the public domain is therefore to a large extent a debate between politicians of the various parties who then come to form a Truth without a major role of the majority of the population. Political parties themselves are a public domain for the politicians of the particular party. An individual politician has to look for solutions for society's problems from the preconditions of the ideology of the political party. If a politician no longer reasons from the ideology of the party then he is left with the option to step out of the party and create his own party or by defecting to an established party with a different ideology.

Deviating opinions are mostly excluded from the public domain before their validity can be tested. In this way renewal is crushed before it even surfaces. A large degree of consensus is present that the current truth is the only correct truth and that there is no need for 'revolutionary' ideas. The problem with this is that there often is no need for new ideas before these ideas exists. For example there was no need for Internet before it existed while no-one can live without it today. This also applies to political ideas. The ruling political elite has vested interest in preventing the rise of new political ideologies and parties because it would undermine their position. The political establishment therefore supports the status quo where it comes to political ideologies. Besides the support of the establishment it is also the Enlightenment principles that lie at the foundation of our democracy which are responsible for the fact that the old ideas still dominate the debate in the public domain. These theories, from socialism to liberalism, are best suited for an environment in which the Enlightenment principles are absolute because their values are derivatives of it.

Modern political parties generally have two distinct functions. The first function is to mobilise the people and to convince them that the ideology the party promotes is correct. The multitude of parties uncovers differences present in the population and partially creates these oppositions as well. The political party that is able to convince the population the most will receive the majority of votes. This is the appearance of the political party as a missionary organisation. The second function of a political party is to govern. The appearance of the political party as bureaucratic organisation. This function is in many respects the opposite of the first function because instead of emphasising differences the political party has to govern on the basis of rules that are applicable to all. In everyday practice this usually means that when a political party has received its votes on the ticket of a specific promise and ideology it will throw these principles out the window and will focus on power politics. Political parties are therefore more often a way to recruit and educate future political leaders than that they are representative for the population. Bureaucratisation of politics is therefore also a sign that the political establishment has no need to convince the people of the legitimacy of their dominance because it is taken for granted.

One of the main tasks of political parties is to uncover and create differences in order to have a truly democratic debate whereby it is possible to discover new truths. It is therefore senseless to claim that a political party should not be allowed to exclude groups, lifestyles or ideas. Prioritizing one thing over the other in order to create the best possible society is one of the pillars of the democratic system.

In the battle for political power it must be assumed that politicians don't primarily operate from the perspective of the people's best interest, but from their own best interest. In case politicians don't identify with the population than democracy disappears.

The public debate is thus primarily controlled by politicians who strive for power and a good career and who have to do this in political parties with distinct ideologies. This in itself is already a limitation of the democratic level of modern democracies. The true democratic deficit however goes beyond that. An environment with power hungry politicians basing their actions and visions on party ideologies is not necessarily undemocratic. Citizens still have the choice what political party they wish to support and anyone is able to establish his own party. Unfortunately, this is mostly theoretical. Virtually all political parties have a long history and new parties usually quickly disappear. Most political parties have ideologies like socialism, liberalism and conservatism that are mainly rooted in the 19th century. The fact that these parties are so long-lived can indicate that the ideas upon which they are founded are good. It could also be that political parties use their power to exclude others and organise the public domain in such a way as to favour the establishment. Furthermore, the will of the people is often manipulated and finally it is also the case that the public domain essentially is an Enlightenment environment that favours the established parties.

To some it appears as if political parties have no ideology and only operate on the basis of *realpolitk*. An example to back this idea is the big difference between present-day socialism and the same ideology thirty years ago. There is undoubtedly a major difference between socialism, liberalism and conservatism now and in the past but this doesn't mean that the ideology has disappeared. The ideologies have not disappeared but they changed to better fit current day society. This indicates that the general public has an impact on the interpretation of the ideologies. It also indicates that the public domain is for a significant part to be found within political parties because much of the change has occurred through internal debate on how to renew the party. Political parties have the monopoly on the most important government positions which provides them with great power to manipulate the public opinion. Combined with the fact that the political debate in the public domain is primarily waged by politicians as well as the tendency of people to vote for people they know means that it is very difficult for new parties to arise and become part of the political landscape.

The way in which the political leadership in a democracy is checked is through voting them out of office when they have implemented bad policy. It might appear reasonable to vote the political leadership out of office in order for the people to have control over the policy that they want to have implemented. Although it is correct that this threat means that the political elite has to take the opinions of the population in mind it is unfortunately not the case that the people control the politicians. As we noted previously the objective of the democratic process is that through a debate people come to a Truth and that this truth consequently is implemented by appointed/elected officials. The people's representatives in a democracy have a certain power but this power is dependent on what they say and do. An important question in this is what representation means.

There are two different definitions of representation when it comes to democracy. The first form of representation is delegation whereby the representative reflects and literally executes the wishes of the to-be-represented group. The second form of representation is different. It is possible for a representative to be a reflection of the group he represents without him being a mere messenger of the group. It is similar to a painting of a landscape which is a reflection of that landscape without it being a copy of it. Instead it enables a truth to be seen that is objectively not present. It creates a truth. This is also how much of the representation works in politics. The truth which is present in politics is partly created by the politicians themselves. Political parties and politicians try to gain power in the public domain. To this end they try to uncover feelings present in the population and subsequently name and manipulate them. The reason why people are searching for a truth is that it hasn't been found yet. There is therefore a sense of vagueness and indeterminateness in the public domain. This vagueness causes insecurity and fear among the population. The best way to handle this fear and insecurity is by labeling the danger, because it is difficult fighting shadows. It is unfair to brush away the fear for societal shadows as irrational, because shadows can be dangerous. We just don't know which ones are dangerous and which are harmless. Uncovering and labeling problems is therefore a crucial part of the task of a politician, because vague and indeterminate feelings present in the population become a reality through this labelling. The fact that politics plays a big role in creating the truth causes a system whereby the population judges its politicians afterwards to be by definition unreliable. How can it be possible to judge a politician whether his actions were good in the sense that they were in accordance with the truth as the best interests of the population, when it is in large part the politician himself who is responsible for creating this truth? Herein lies an ideal element for abuse and misuse by politicians that is eagerly used by them. As we noted previously the most important motivation of politicians is to gain power. It is therefore relatively easy to legitimate political manipulation because it is an integral part of a system that is seen by most to be legitimate and perhaps not perfect but the least bad one of all.

Liberalism

Liberalism states that a government which forces its people to be free is in reality a dictatorship. According to liberalism, helping the oppressed and marginalized, as socialism calls for, can therefore not be a policy of the state. As opposed to socialism, liberalism prioritizes the freedom of the state's citizens to organize their own life without hindrance from other people or the state. The liberal ideology is therefore especially attractive to the elite because they have the resources to be free of oppression. The fact that this usually comes at the expense of others who are then not free is thereby ignored.

Liberalism assumes atomised individuals who rationally interact with the world. We noted previously that people are not atomised individuals and that rationality based on the individual is both unfair to society and to the person himself. Furthermore, it is scientifically incorrect. When we are confronted with injustice in the event that others take more than their fair share, than our sense of justice becomes stronger than our self-interest. Such feelings are innately human and necessary to survive in a human group. The responses from the test subjects in the ultimatum game show us that people don't act rationally from their individual self-interest but that they act from the interest of the Self. This is a crucial characteristic because if people were truly creatures that rationally acted out of individual self-interest than cooperation would be impossible without external oppression. Fortunately, the psychological make-up of people is directed at fair cooperation, meaning that there is more freedom possible than in a liberal system.

The idea that liberal democracy is the end-station of human history is therefore a strange and senseless statement, because liberalism does not correspond to scientific research that has been done into the way people interpret the world and their innate human nature. Liberalism should instead be seen as a theory that has been proven false. The basic unit from which we should build society should not be the individual but the Self. The Self includes the physical person and *an* environment. It is important to note that the Self includes *an* environment and not *the* environment. Through selectively choosing what environment belongs to the Self and what not, we can arrive at completely different outcomes. In light of the fact that the environment can also include abstract ideals, inanimate objects and just about everything we can identify with makes it difficult to predict what the precise content of the Self will be.

Individualism is not an end in itself but a means to get a good social position within a group. Liberalism is often used by the elite to legitimize and rationalize its own privileged position. An important characteristic of liberalism is to minimize the influence of the state. Liberalism assumes that people approach the world from an individualistic self-interest and that this leads to a competitive society in which the primary objective of the state is to make sure that people don't harm the other too much and that individual freedom is protected. A liberal state is therefore primarily a law-and-order government that ensures peace and stability in order for people to organise their personal lives in freedom. An ideological state should than be avoided because that would limit the freedom of its citizens. From a liberal perspective the ideal state should therefore be a-moral. A major problem in this is that there is no possibility for identification with each other or with the state. The state is not intended to promote the best interest of the community but its only purpose is to protect individuals from other individuals. In liberalism neighbours are enemies while the state is only a referee. The citizen then becomes a client. Besides the fact that liberalism paints an incorrect image of people and the way in which politics works, it also alienates citizens from the government. In liberalism government is no longer under the control of the citizens. Citizenship has then disappeared and people have become clients. If the state is not allowed to have an ideological policy, but only acts to ensure peace and stability than politics is no longer needed because there is already a Truth. This truth is to maintain order. In the event that the government would be completely liberal, it follows that it would also be completely detached from the people. The *people* would in fact stop to exist because there would only be a collection of individuals who have nothing in common with each other than being subject to the same state. A liberal state is therefore high-jacked by an elite which does not identify with the people. The fact that people are not atomised individuals but despite this are treated that way creates a lot of despair and insecurity among the population. People become alienated from each other and are no longer represented by the state. Liberalism is therefore mainly a method of the elite to have the people think that it is in their best interest to be individualistic and to focus on individual freedom while in reality the elite is the only one that profits. This is best visible in so called 'neo-liberal' policy whereby the focus is on a completely free market (for capital) and globalisation. On many occasions liberalism has been declared absolute after the fall of communism and the Soviet Union. Unfortunately liberalism proved to be mostly a euphemism for socialism for the rich.

Liberal ideology was frequently used in the past to break community consensus. The problem with neo-liberalism is that it assumes that liberalism should be placed as the foundation of a new consensus. We noted previously that rationality not originates in the individual but in the Self. To build a system on the basis of rationally thinking individuals would mean that we build a system that is inhuman and denies human nature. In the event that we don't build a system to fit human nature but try to adapt people to fit a theoretical ideal then we create an inhuman system and endanger human survival. Fortunately, people are flexible and are able to adapt to different situations. It is however not possible to transcend human nature and go from a rationality of the Self to a rationality of the individual. Human flexibility then focuses on changing the behavioural patterns and identification in such a way that there is still the need for identification and sense of community but that this need is narrowed to include only part of society. Society then breaks up in smaller groups whereby identification only encompasses small groups and all others are perceived as enemies. This is the way in which a small group of industry leaders and bankers awarded themselves huge rewards legitimating it by pointing to market forces, while these forces were present everywhere except in the top.

Liberalism is however not all bad even though it is based on principles that have been proven false. It offers the possibility to break the current consensus and thereby to search for a new truth. We noted previously that people have the tendency to conform to persons and a group with whom we identify. Furthermore, there is a difference between the people with whom we identify and the others who are de-humanized. These Others are outside the Self and therefore also outside morality. This can lead to corruption in our modern society because only 'our kind of people' are helped while the others are seen as enemies and therefore excluded. Liberalism is able to break the bonds within these small groups leading to a decrease in corruption. When this is combined with a new (nationalist or socialist) ideology that recognizes everyone as equals then morality will encompass all and a new consensus will be created. This equality implies a form of socialism. Liberalism is therefore not a stable form of social organisation and will always decay to a more human variety, i.e. a form of (national-)socialism. Liberalism doesn't just break socialism but it also makes socialism possible.

The origins of democracy

A modern free society enables people to display their innate natural behaviour as it has evolved in human evolution. An important question then arises is whether democracy is part of human nature or differently put are the underlying principles of democracy part of human nature? If democracy is something innately human then it will be inevitable in human social evolution and can we expect the world to become democratic whether we pursue it or not. When we jump to the conclusion we see that it is not inevitable that a modern society becomes democratic and that other aspects play a role that determine the viability of democracy. It is also possible that democracy is part of human nature but that modern society can sometimes place such demands on people that it is not achievable or even desirable. It can also be the case that democratic principles are not part of human nature but that they were invented by the ancient Greeks. An important part of the European cultural and especially philosophical heritage is based on the writings of the ancient Greeks during the times of Socrates, Plato and Aristotle. Ancient Greece had a form of democracy in which all free men of the city-state could participate in decisions about important policy. Public debate played an important role and therefore had high status. Ancient Greece did not know printed media or television like we have in our modern democracy. The participation of citizens in forming ideas and policy could therefore only be done by the physical presence of people in the public arena. The size of the group in which democracy was played out was therefore limited. The Greek city-states still had several hundred-thousand inhabitants and although only a small proportion consisted of free men they already had a form of representation. Modern democracies in Europe and America are far more advanced than those in ancient Greece but are still based on the same pillars, like the establishment of a public domain where through debate people come to a truth that subsequently is implemented by a representative. 25 centuries ago the large amount of freedom and equality that is necessary to let the democratic system function was also present in ancient Greece but not in the other developed agricultural communities of the time. This could be an argument to trace democracy to ancient Greece and not to human nature, but this would ignore the fact that the demands of democracy, like freedom and equality, were also present in pre-history. By looking at the degree of freedom and equality from a historical perspective we see that the 21st century has a lot of both. Industrial- and agricultural societies were strongly hierarchical, while hunter/gatherer cultures also had a large degree of freedom and equality. The age of ancient Greece was an era in which agricultural societies were dominant. From this perspective we can trace the uniqueness of ancient Greece to the fact that it was able to create a relatively free public domain and have a democracy even though societal structures tended towards hierarchy and dictatorship. It is important to note that Greek democracy did not spread to other regions and also didn't last in Greece itself. This was most likely due to the fact that democracy was not an effective way to govern ancient agricultural societies. The modern age changed the circumstances and enables the natural tendencies of people to be displayed in a democratic polity. The fact that the success of democratic systems depends on the form of society shows that in the future technological and social innovations might take place that are not conducive to democracy. Perhaps the future will give rise to other ways of social organisation whereby decisions will be taken differently.

People are the product of a long evolution. During most of this process people lived as hunter/gatherers in a small group. The physical and mental make-up of people can therefore be traced to this era. We know that hunter/gatherers had a great degree of freedom and equality and that they didn't have dictatorial leadership but that decisions were the result of debate in the group. Not all agreed with the eventual consensus in the group and so leaders within the groups arose who represented the incomplete consensus thereby also imposing it to others who had a different opinion. The same applies in current democratic politics. The basic characteristics that enable modern democracy to function can therefore be traced to human evolution in hunter/gatherer groups.

There are many arguments that point to a natural origin of democracy. With this is meant that there are innate human characteristics that prefer democracy over other forms of social organisation. These are of course not absolute truths from the laws of physics, but they do however find there origin in human morality. The state of human nature makes for the fact that the democratic principles are rooted in innate human characteristics. Firstly there is the fact that a person is not an atomised individual and that a person can never be complete on his own. Instead we noted that the Self provides a better description of people. The environment and other persons are than also part of the Self. This overlap and identification lies at the basis of cooperation between people and is therefore also applicable to democracy. We noted that people are by nature not directed at hard, individualistic competition but that they are very conformist towards those with which we identify. There is therefore no natural tendency to hold power over others because this would be a form of oppression of our-Self. Instead, there is a natural tendency towards freedom and equality. People do not approach the world from an individualistic perspective but instead do this from the perspective of the Self. We noted previously that rationality originates in the Self and not the individual. Because social- and political science don't see this difference people wrongly assume that certain decisions are taken irrationally while they are in fact rational from the perspective of the Self. This is also true when looking at the support for politicians and political parties. People are by nature both emotional as rational. The fact that rationality originates in the Self and not in the individual makes democracy possible. In that sense there is an innate ability to support democracy. The public domain is only possible when we look at people as a person who identifies with others and thereby recognizing them as equal. Unfortunately, also oligarchy can be traced to innate human characteristics. In an oligarchy an elite monopolises the resources of society at the expense of the larger population. Oligarchy is probably closer to human nature because an oligarchy is based on democracy within a limited group of equals whereby all those who are not part of the group are de-humanized. In the discussion on liberalism we noted that this is caused by the fact that identification is limited to a small group instead of the entire society. Nationalism can broaden this identification. Due to the fact that there is no morality outside the Self means that violence against the Others in society is not immoral if society consists of multiple groups that don't identify with each other. These observations combined with the fact that for example agricultural societies tend to lean towards anti-democratic structures indicates that we can't say that society will inevitably become democratic because it just happens to be facilitated by human nature. Other social forms of organisation also have their basis in certain aspects of human nature. The best thing that we can currently say is that the present technological developments are conducive to democracy and enable us to live closely to our innate abilities as developed through millennia of evolution as hunter/gatherers. When we ensure that everyone is able to identify with each other and avoid the presence of zero sum competition than democracy is the most viable structure for society in our era. It is also true that everyone with which we don't share identification is placed outside the community and outside morality, meaning that democracy is limited to those with whom we identify.

The democratic deficit

The debate that takes place in the public domain clearly shows that this environment is everything but free of moral values. An important objective of a debate is to win over the other on the basis of arguments. Of course this can never be free of value because the objective is to convince the other of your position. Whether people choose to be convinced by the arguments depends on the fact if they are deemed more valuable or more ethically correct. As we noted previously, nature knows no objective or values and only consists of facts and events. If we were to focus solely on the facts there would be no possibility to decide which facts are more important and why. This makes it essential that the democratic process is filled with values, but also states that the end product of the democratic process is value-laden as well. The power in a democracy therefore has strong connections with the dominant values in society. Power is more dispersed in a democracy than in a dictatorship and it is often difficult to pinpoint the location of it. This doesn't mean that there are no persons or groups who have more power than others. Despite these differences the power of the elite is different in a democracy than in a dictatorship. The power of the elite is in large part delegated to them by the population. Ideally the people's representatives obtain their power by convincing the population that they are best able to further their interests. This is not a one-time process but a continuous interaction between the arguments of the representatives and the interests of the population. In an ideal democracy, power is than not in the hands of the political elite but is present everywhere. In light of the fact that the most important objective of politicians is to gain power and that they need to do this through debate in the public domain leads to the conclusion that there is no such thing as an objective search for truth, but that the participants in the public domain will use every means necessary to bend the truth to suit their best interests.

An essential part of democracy is that people come to a truth through the process of a debate and that representatives are appointed to carry out this truth. The people's representatives in a democracy have some power but this power is dependent on what they say and do. The question than is what is meant by representation? We can make a distinction in the meaning of representation with one form being delegation. The to-be-represented party is hereby reflected in the delegation whereby the latter executes exactly what the people want. Another form of representation can be compared to a painting of a landscape. Such a painting is a representation of the landscape. It is however not an exact copy but an interpretation. A painting makes a truth visible that would otherwise not be visible or present. The latter form of representation is the one that is present in politics. The truth that the political elite represents has been partly created by them. Politicians and political parties try to gain power in the public arena. To this end they try to find, name and manipulate feelings and interests in the general population. The reason that people are looking for a truth lies in the fact that it hasn't been found yet. This causes feelings of uncertainty and indeterminateness to be present in the public domain. This uncertainty in turn creates fear and anxiety in the population. The best way to cope with this fear of uncertainty is to name the danger, because it is difficult fighting shadows. It is unfair to dismiss the fear for the shadows in society as irrational, because shadows can be dangerous. Not every shadow is dangerous, but any shadow can be. Naming problems is therefore a crucial part of the task of a politician, because naming a problem causes a certain indeterminate feeling that is present in the population to become reality. The fact that politics plays such a major role in the creation of the truth causes a system in which politicians have to afterwards account for their actions unreliable and undemocratic. How can it be possible to judge a politician based on the truth of society, meaning if his decisions were right or wrong, when it is in large part the politician himself who is responsible for the creation of that truth? Herein lies an ideal element for abuse and it is therefore relatively easy to legitimate political manipulation, because it is an integrated part of a system that is seen by the majority as a good and legitimate system.

The idea that the power in a democracy is in the hands of the people because the political elite is dependent on the opinions that are formed in the public domain are misleading and false. It is almost exclusively the political and social elite who are the ones participating in the public debate because they monopolise all positions of power and therefore control the direction and outcome of the debate.

It is therefore important for democracy to be truly democratic to have the political elite see themselves as part of the people and not an elite. An open society for the entire population as well as freedom and equality for all are essential for a true democracy. A society in which an elite governs also means that the will of the population has been manipulated and uncivilization is imposed. In light of the fact that this manipulation leads people to desire things that go against their best interests makes it important that this oppression is dealt with. A purely populist way of doing politics whereby politicians simply act on what the population desires does not lead to a decrease of the democratic deficit but instead strengthens it. Freeing the will of the people, increasing self-confidence of people and recognition of each other is important. However we should also look beyond the ideology that governs society. We should not look at the world in such a way that we go to every effort so as not to see what is obvious and in plain sight because it doesn't fit our ideological assumptions. Fooling ourselves will undermine the potential of society and endanger the eventual objective of life, meaning our survival.

An important argument within democratic theory is the principle that there should be free access to the public domain, which means that society should guarantee a large degree of freedom and equality. When this freedom and equality are threatened then there is an attack on democracy itself. Many political scientists assume that when freedom is under threat, resistance is not only justified but even obligatory because democracy itself would else be destroyed. Such a prescription is valid in case of a foreign occupation force that suspends democracy and freedom. It is however also valid for an internal occupation. As we noted in the discussion on the open society this society can be closed off for a section of the people by the elite. The population can also be excluded from the public domain and thereby placed outside the political debate, which indicates that democracy is no longer applicable to them. A part of the population is then placed outside the Self of the elite and they have become de-humanized Others. They are therefore oppressed and no longer represented in the democratic procedures. An example of this is South Africa during the days of Apartheid. Apartheid South Africa was a democracy in which the democracy was for the whites and the oppression for all the others. It was therefore completely legitimate from the perspective of the oppressed to resist the Apartheid regime even though it was democratic for 'its own' people. Something similar is also visible in many other countries whereby there is democracy for a part of the population but not for the rest. Such a situation implies that violence is legitimate and even proscribed. How this violence should be implemented is then the only remaining question.

The social contract

An important collection of theories to explain and justify human cooperation in groups is called the social contract theory. This theory assumes that individuals form a contract with each other and thereby create a social organisation that transcends the individual. Every cooperation is than the result of a social contract which all the individual members have signed. Although the ancient Greeks already thought about social contracts the most important historical thinkers about the modern social contract theory are Thomas Hobbes (1651), John Locke (1689), Jean-Jacques Rousseau (1762) and John Rawls (1971). Each of these philosophers has formulated his own version of the social contract which will be described below.

Thomas Hobbes

Thomas Hobbes lived during the 16th and 17th century in England in a period of constant wars, both nationally as internationally. In 1651 he published a book called Leviathan in which he unfolded his social contract theory. According to Hobbes people are driven by their emotions and not by any form of rationality. These emotions can be organised in two categories: pleasure (good) and pain (bad). Human happiness is than a continuous repetition of pleasure. The most important emotions that according to Hobbes are at the basis of all human actions are the desire for power and fear of a violent death. Furthermore, he stated that this drive for power would eventually lead to death and never to a situation of peace and tranquillity. People in their state of nature are continuously afraid of others who they see as potential killers. This fear is a motivation to seek more power, which in turn leads to fear in others who see this as a threat to their existence. This vicious circle of fear and violence in which everyone is trying to get peace and tranquillity for himself by striving for power thereby striking fear in others who subsequently strive for power as well, can only be broken by erecting an all powerful state that can impose peace and stability on everyone.

The state of nature of people is according to Hobbes not historic but something natural and innate and is always lurking deep within us. Individuals are unable to guarantee their own safety and therefore a contract whereby the rights are laid down and implemented by a powerful state is necessary. This government is above the people and leads them to a common goal. The legitimacy of the existence of the state is the protection it offers; the stronger the state, the higher the legitimacy. The state itself is not part of the social contract and therefore not bound by it. The legitimacy of the contract depends on the measure in which the state can guarantee safety and security to its citizens. According to Hobbes the state of nature of people is one in which everyone is at war with the other and where according to Hobbes: "human existence is lonely, poor, mean, brutish and short". In order to escape from human nature individuals sign a contract to erect an all powerful state that imposes peace and stability.

This social contract theory is very different from the viewpoints in this book. Firstly, Hobbes takes the individual as the building block for his theory while this can not be correct. The basic element of a political theory should not be the individual but, as we noted in the previous pages, the Self. Taking into account that the Self is not limited to the physical individual means that a sound social contract theory will look completely different than Hobbes' one. The state of nature of people can never be so violent towards the other because the other is in fact part of the Self.

Hobbes does correctly state that the foundation for human motivation lies in their emotions and not in rational thinking. Morality of people is for the most part innate whereby a distinction is made between the morality for one's own people and for the outsiders. Morality is not really applicable to the latter because there is no morality beyond the Self. Furthermore, people are by nature not inclined to hurt and kill others in their environment who belong to the Self. There is on the contrary a strong drive to conform to the norms and values of the group. The state of nature of people is therefore not violent but easy-going. The state of nature here means the innate capabilities and tendencies of people as how they would be played out when there would be no external force that pushes people to behave in a certain way. What Hobbes thought to recognize as the state of human nature was in reality a breakdown of the social environment and thereby a breakdown of the state of human nature.

Hobbes also states that people sign a contract as individuals when they are in their state of human nature and therefore in a war of all against all. In light of the fact that according to Hobbes they are in a state of war, the morality that would be necessary to give the social contract its value is absent, because there are no obligations. This is a classic chicken-and-the-egg problem. Before you can sign a contract there needs to be a morality present that gives the contract its value, but according to Hobbes morality only starts after the contract has been signed. In later pages we will see that the chicken-and-the-egg problem can be solved when we take the Self as building block instead of the individual.

Another argument that can be used against all the social contract theories is the question why the contract should be applicable to present day people when it was our ancestors who signed the contract. Furthermore, it is possible to cancel a normal contract while it is not possible to cancel the social contract. The social contract can of course also be seen as a theoretical contract, but that would raise the question what the practical value of such a contract would be because a hypothetical contract only binds hypothetical persons and not real-life people.

Another point that Hobbes addresses is the role of the state. According to Hobbes the state should offer besides security also a common goal. Hobbes sees the state therefore correctly as a moral entity and not a scientific a-moral institution. Unfortunately his vision is anti-democratic and an almighty state which stands above the people and is based on imposing peace and stability will result in the exact opposite of what Hobbes' theory states. Such a state is high-jacked by the elite and has become an enemy of the people. It provides peace and security for the elite at the expense of all those who are subjects of the state.

John Locke

The social contract theory of John Locke is somewhat different from Hobbes' theory. Locke does not present his theory of the state of human nature as being a war of all against all, but as a much friendlier situation in which peace and stability, mutual recognition and individual freedom can be found. According to Locke, the state of human nature is characterised by a situation of complete equality and individual freedom where the laws of nature are applicable. People are by nature good and the social contract is therefore not based on fear of the other but on expansion of personal possibilities. The social contract is an agreement between free and equal persons who decide in freedom to leave the state of human nature behind and erect a political entity. A good government therefore needs permission of the people, meaning that the majority should rule. This is accomplished by emphasising the authority of institutions and freedom under the law. Persons are equal under the law, but there is no material equality. Locke states that class differences are good and should be protected. Furthermore, Locke states that the most important legitimacy of the state to make and enforce laws is to protect, guarantee and regulate the possession of private property. When the state disowns people or hinders them in using their private property in the best possible way than there is a right to rebel against the state. According to Locke this is the only legitimate reason to question the state.

Locke too assumes that individuals in their state of nature sign a contract with others. The previous comment, that the unit of organisation is not the individual but the Self, also fatally undermines Locke's theory. The idea that people are by nature good is however correct if we limit it to all those who are part of the Self. Locke also states that the state should be legitimated by the majority of the people. This caused the theory of Locke to have a much greater influence than Hobbes' theory on how to best establish and organise modern democracies. The freedom of all under the law and the great importance that the theory bestows on the regulating of private property are important pillars of modern, democratic and especially capitalist societies. The defence and promotion of class differences however undermine the democratic contents of society. A class society creates a system in which there is an open society for the few at the top, while the lower classes are imprisoned in a closed society where the rules of uncivilization are in force.

Jean Jacques Rousseau

The social contract theory of Jean Jacques Rousseau has elements of the theory of Hobbes and of Locke as well as completely new ideas. Rousseau believes that people in their state of nature are atomised individuals who are neither good nor bad according to present morality and who live isolated without social bonds. A person lives according to his natural instincts without fear of death. Property does not exist in the state of human nature, everyone is equal and the basic human motivations are compassion for the other and love for himself. At a specific moment in history people saw the necessity to cooperate and left the state of nature to form a permanent society. Since that time the possibility of ever returning to the state of human nature are ruled out. The social relations in society go against human nature and are the cause of many socially created diseases. Property is unnatural as are class differences. Power and the will to gain power are also a product of the culture and not of nature, which causes both the master and the slave to be a victim of desires that are unnatural and that keep social insecurity alive. Due to the fact that we wish to satisfy unnatural desires we have to act against our conscience, leading to selfishness. Although there is no possibility to return to the state of human nature we are able to partially mend the rupture. This can be done by education and by grounding politics on a moral foundation. All individual freedom has to be transferred to the state whereby the happiness of the individual is absorbed and becomes part of the happiness of society as a whole. The happiness of the individual is therefore only possible if society as a whole knows happiness, resulting in the situation in which the promotion of self-interest automatically promotes the general good. We thereby transcend our selfishness and become moral beings again which we already were in the state of human nature, but now with the ability to live in a modern society. According to Rousseau the political authority is in the hands of the general will and not like with Locke in the hands of the majority. In the political society of Rousseau everyone is subject to the general will. Furthermore, factions are illegal as are differences between rich and poor. Rousseau also states that society can not become too large because political representation is not allowed; only direct representation is allowed.

Similar to Hobbes and Locke, Rousseau also bases his theory on the assumption that people are atomised individuals and from this natural state sign a social contract. As we noted previously a contract signed in an a-moral environment can never have value. The vision of Rousseau is similar to the Christian story of creation. Rousseau sees an ideal living environment from which people are banned because at one specific moment in time they decided to form an alliance with others after which a return is never possible. This is comparable with the expulsion out of the Garden of Eden after man committed a sin. Rousseau implies in his theory that mankind fell from grace. The results are that people desire things that are unnatural and go against their conscience. Similar to

Hobbes, Rousseau also sees the state as all-powerful but from a more benign perspective. Unfortunately, the idea of an absolute authority of the general will is an important idea of any totalitarian state in which every deviation and all individual behaviour is outlawed. Such a view of the state is very destructive to society because it hinders the ability of people to adapt to a continuously changing situation thereby degrading the potential flexibility and creativity of society. The dominant rule of the general will is thereby also problematic, because who determines what this general will exactly is if everyone is bound by and a subject of it? The idea is therefore ideally suited for abuse by a dictator. In order to ban selfishness no differences between rich and poor are allowed and also factions are illegal. It is indeed very important to not allow major differences in society else people will not be able to identify with each other and a situation will arise in which the other is no longer part of morality. This does not mean that there can be no difference at all, as Rousseau might propose, but that the difference should be limited and not durable. Something similar applies to the factions in Rousseau's theory. Rousseau states the undesirability of different political parties or factions that compete with each other. According to Rousseau this competition undermines the social contract. This is incorrect because it is possible to have competing political parties that all claim to have the right vision on how to organise society in such a way that people are better able to choose how they want the world to be organised. The idea that political representation is always bad is also an incorrect vision of democracy. The general will might appear to be democratic but there are some important differences. Democratic theory presumes that you are able to choose representatives who then execute the desired policy as good as possible. These representatives can also implement policy which is too complex and all encompassing to be fully 'desired' by the people because they lack the expertise. It is of great importance that the political representatives identify with the people they represent. In that sense there is not a general will in a democratic society but more a general identification or a 'general Self'.

John Rawls

John Rawls was a 20th century philosopher who has also been important in the debate about social contracts. Rawls does not base his theory on the state of human nature but on a hypothetical thought experiment to test if society is fair. In order to do this Rawls places hypothetical persons behind a veil of ignorance from where they have to decide on the kind of principles society should be based upon. With this 'veil of ignorance' is meant that people don't know what skills or future social position they will have after they become part of society. According to Rawls we should organize a just and fair society by making rational decisions from an 'original position' behind the veil of ignorance. From this process two principles would follow that together describe a just society. The first principle is the idea that all persons should have freedom as long as that freedom doesn't limit others in their freedom. The second principle states that economic distribution should be organized in such a way so that inequalities would also benefit the less well off and that everyone should be able to get any job in society. Social differences are therefore allowed as long as the least well off profit the most. Furthermore, the first principle is more important and takes precedence over the second principle.

The theory of Rawls had great influence on the justification of social-democratic policies. This influence comes despite the fact that there are many problems with the theory. First, it simply does not take human nature into account but instead offers a purely theoretical ideal. A legitimate question would of course be why the theory would hold that people will choose freedom and economic distribution that favours the least well off? Perhaps this is not what people wish and if they would want it than the theory is still not a rational explanation for it. Furthermore, Rawls also assumes the existence of atomised individuals without social bonds. There is also no explanation on why there would even be cooperation. Also the fact that Rawls claims to seek justice through rational decisions is not in accordance with reality. Rawls assumes that morality is rational, while the basis for it is in fact our emotions. It's the emotions that form the foundation for morality and they in the end determine what is just and what is not. Without our emotions it is impossible to distinguish good from bad. The theory of Rawls does not state why people make these choices, because no definition on the state of human nature is given. Rawls theory does not describe the state of human nature and uses only hypothetical persons which leaves the theory without foundation and ultimately makes it useless, because it does not provide an explanation or a justification for the principles that Rawls thinks to recognize.

A new social contract theory

In previous pages we saw the different social contract theories and concluded that none of them provides an accurate description of reality. All four theories take the atomised individual as the elementary building block of a social contract theory, while it should be the Self that is used as elementary building block. A social contract based on the Self and not the individual provides for a morality that is already present when signing the contract. The chicken-and-the-egg problem is thus avoided. The social contract has to take human limitations into consideration, among which is the impossibility of morality outside the Self. The impossibility of morality beyond the Self forces people to increase their recognition and identification with each other in such a way that everyone that has signed the social contract becomes part of the Self. This implies that everyone should be treated as yourself and as an equal, meaning that major social differences can't be allowed. The existence of durable (ethnic) groups is therefore not allowed. If durable differences were to be allowed than we would not have one society but many competing groups. The widespread corruption and violence in countries which lack identification within the entire population is a good example of the devastating consequences of such a lack of identification.

In a competitive environment it is only possible to be tolerant if the other does not have a durable more successful strategy because else you die out. The objective of life is simply survival. Forces in society can however push certain groups into a position where they forget this simple fact of life. People and lifestyles are tolerated as long as they are not seen as a threat, meaning that the to-be-tolerated strategy should be less favourable to survival. In the event that it does enhance survival there should be the possibility to adopt this strategy. For example, the tolerance for homosexuality declines when identification becomes too great. In many instances people do not wish to take over their strategy but the increased emancipation does encourage it, because as we noted previously, there is no morality outside the Self, meaning that emancipation tries to bring others into the Self of the general public. In order to alleviate this pressure, people become less tolerant towards homosexuality. A solution for this intolerance is to partly de-humanize the other and to see him on certain points as not completely human whereby the identification lessens. The other is than a person who lacks certain essential skills and characteristics making him not fully human. People are than partly de-humanized. In the case of homosexuality this means that their extravagant lifestyle can be directly connected to the fact that they are gay. When such a connection is made absolute, meaning that the two are directly associated with each other, than homosexuality is accepted as long as the characteristics are not part of one's own lifestyle. It is than possible to live next to each other as long as the other not directly competes for the same scarce resources. A major problem in this is the fact that a gay lifestyle is created that is only gay because people do not want to be associated with them and not because of any objective link between homosexuality and an extravagant lifestyle. This extravagant lifestyle is than no longer accessible to others who are not gay, because the direct association with homosexuality means that everyone is excluded who takes over part of 'their' lifestyle. This implies a major limitation to the generally accepted lifestyle of ordinary people. In case multiple groups are present in society with which people don't want to be associated than the generally accepted lifestyle can quickly become very slim, because people don't want to identify completely with the other. A pluralist society of different durable groups living next to each other is therefore a limitation for all. Due to the fact that lifestyles can be associated with groups that people don't want to be part of means that this lifestyle and its possible better insights for survival are closed off. The possibility to escape a limited lifestyle increases when the competition and number of groups decreases. There is than the possibility to have a slightly different lifestyle without the risk of being excluded from the group. All individual lives can in this way be enriched as can society as a whole. Furthermore, increased identification increases freedom because there will no longer be a need for external force to impose cooperation.

Modern society is based on a social contract and, as we noted in previous pages, the building blocks of this contract are the Self of each person. Through identification with each other it is possible to live together in one society without the need for an external power to impose freedom. This is contrary to the theory of Hobbes and to the theory of liberalism. Mutual identification creates and perpetuates the public domain causing modern democracy to be wholly dependent upon a healthy social contract. This is therefore one of the most important reasons why a social contract is necessary. According to Hobbes the reasons for the social contract are to guarantee safety for individual citizens; according to Locke the reason for the social contract is to be found in the possibility to increase the potential of each individual and Rousseau sees the social contract as caused by a one-time error of judgment when people thought there was a need to cooperate after which they are forever imprisoned. The interpretation of the social contract based on the Self shows that the contract is not a fixed document that was signed once but that it is continuously worked on. The question if a social contract is also applicable to a person in the 21st century if it was signed by distant ancestors is therefore the wrong question because the contract is signed continuously. Although it is true that we build on the achievements of our ancestors, exactly how we organize present day society is dependent on our current interpretations of what our ancestors have left us. In doing so we have to be aware that habitual behaviour is very strong and that previous behaviours and lines of thought might have been appropriate at one time in the past but that they can be harmful in our present era.

Democracy is highly dependent on a well functioning public domain. The public domain can be monopolised by an elite who can than exclude new ideas and cultural innovations that might jeopardise their reign. The public domain includes the political debate and also the accepted norms and values of all those who participate in the public arena. These accepted norms and values are not so much determined by the numerical majority but by the majority in the public domain. This makes it possible for a loud and powerful minority to become a majority in the public domain whereby they are able to determine the contents of the social contract. It is therefore not the general will of Rousseau or the physical majority of Locke that determines how the social contract is implemented but it's the powerful in the public domain who set the agenda. The power of the media and political parties can therefore be troublesome. The social contract is founded on the Self and the wish to create a public domain in which a democratic process is possible.

Another question is how a social contract can be cancelled and if it is actually possible. The fact that the social contract is continuously affirmed indicates that it is a dynamic document. By not participating in the political debate and boycotting elections, an important element of the social contract can be unilaterally cancelled. This however does not bring more freedom. When people become silent in the public domain it literally means that they are no longer heard and they can subsequently be ignored letting other people decide on policy decisions. The world will continue to turn and the ruling elite will simply decide what route to follow and those who remain silent are forced to follow. There is therefore nothing to gain by simply falling silent. A possibility to change the social contract to better reflect your interests is to create greater visibility in the public domain. This can be done in the form of an emancipation movement like the equal rights movement. Another option is to display less accepted behaviour in the public domain like rude and criminal behaviour. This call for attention will be heard only when the majority in the public domain gets hurt and/or identifies with the struggle.

Retreating from the public domain and trying to change opinions through violence or lobbying are both directed at renegotiating the social contract instead of truly cancelling it. Emigration is an example of cancelling the social contract whereby all connections are broken and all potential benefits of society are relinquished. Establishment of a parallel society is also an example of cancelling the social contract whereby people are not driven out but where identification is narrowed to a smaller group. Many countries see this narrowing of identities whereby ethnic groups only identify with their own group. These are all the options to cancel the social contract. It is for example impossible to break all bonds with other people and still live a full life. Morality is as important for human survival as oxygen. If the environment is vacuum of values than it is comparable to an environment vacuum of oxygen and thus unliveable for people. It is impossible to remove morality out of the human environment because that would result in an unliveable and inhuman environment.

In conclusion we can state that the social contract can be influenced, changed and even cancelled, but that it is not an easy task because power is so dispersed and the interdependency so great. The social contract is based on the Self and we have seen in previous chapters that people are automatically directed outward whereby others are recognized. In the social contract theory based on the Self the connection between people is therefore innately present, contrary to the theories of Hobbes, Locke, Rousseau and Rawls who all focus on binding individuals to each other. In the new social contract theory it is therefore not the case of binding people together but to make sure that everyone identifies with each other. In a society which makes it impossible for small groups to durably isolate themselves over the generations, this identification comes naturally. The social contract theory based on the Self is not directed at binding people (because that happens naturally) but on preventing the rise and continued existence of durable groups who only identify with each other. Ironically the new social contract theory states that government should focus on breaking inappropriate social connections and not on trying to connect people. If we are successful in doing so we can reach a situation where everyone is connected in a mutual dependence of each other.

Conclusion

If we wish to prosper and survive as humanity than we need to create an environment where our innate capabilities do us justice instead of trying to change people to fit a system. A system not made to fit man's innate abilities would be by definition an immoral system. People are by nature good and well intentioned against all those with whom there is identification and who are thereby part of the Self. Combined with the fact that during every phase of life people have the natural tendency to search for recognition means that the group is always in the process of coming together. There is thus a natural tendency towards integration. When we take down the barriers in our society that prevent mutual identification then innate human tendencies will guarantee a just and peaceful society for all people no matter race or creed. Insights in the philosophy of Ubuntu can help us reach just such a society.

www.ingramcontent.com/pod-product-compliance
Lightning Source LLC
Chambersburg PA
CBHW031236280526
45784CB00004B/1596